TOTAL
SPORTS

DK Publishing

DK

LONDON, NEW YORK,
MELBOURNE, MUNICH, AND DELHI

Project editor Alexander Cox
Senior designer Rachael Grady

US editor Margaret Parrish
Picture researcher Jo Walton
Production editor Sean Daly
Production controller Claire Pearson
Jacket designer Martin Wilson
Jacket editor Matilda Gollon

Publishing manager Bridget Giles
Art director Martin Wilson
Creative director Jane Bull
Publisher Mary Ling

Produced with assistance from Tall Tree Ltd.
Editors Jon Richards and Jennifer Sanderson
Designers Malcolm Parchment and Ed Simkins
Consultant Clive Gifford

First published in the United States in 2011 by
DK Publishing
375 Hudson Street, New York, New York 10014

Copyright © 2011 Dorling Kindersley Limited

11 12 13 14 15   10 9 8 7 6 5 4 3 2 1
001–180847–Jun/11

A catalog record for this book
is available from the Library of Congress.

ISBN: 978-0-7566-8231-6

Printed and bound in China by Toppan

Discover more at
www.dk.com

Contents

6 A SPORT FOR EVERYONE

TEAM SPORTS

10 SOCCER
12 BASEBALL
14 BASKETBALL
16 VOLLEYBALL AND NETBALL
18 FOOTBALL
20 RUGBY UNION
22 AUSTRALIAN RULES
24 ICE HOCKEY AND
    FIELD HOCKEY
26 CRICKET
28 OTHER TEAMS

RACKET SPORTS

32 TENNIS
34 TABLE TENNIS AND BADMINTON
36 SQUASH
38 DIFFERENT RACKETS

TRACK & FIELD AND GYMNASTICS

42 SPRINTING
44 DISTANCE EVENTS
46 JUMPING
48 THROWING
50 WEIGHTLIFTING
52 GYMNASTICS
54 ON THE FLOOR

TARGET SPORTS

58 GOLF
60 CURLING AND BOWLS
62 TEN-PIN
64 SNOOKER AND POOL
66 ARCHERY
68 AIMING HIGH

WATER SPORTS

72 SWIMMING
74 DIVING
76 ROWING AND KAYAKING
78 SAILING
80 WINDSURFING
82 SURFING
84 MORE SPLASH

COMBAT SPORTS

88 BOXING

90 WRESTLING

92 JUDO AND JU JITSU

94 KARATE AND TAEKWONDO

96 FENCING

98 A NEW CHALLENGE

WINTER SPORTS

102 SKIING

104 SNOWBOARDING

106 BOBSLED AND LUGE AND SKELETON

108 SPEED SKATING AND ICE SKATING

110 FRESH SNOW

HORSE SPORTS

114 HORSE RACING AND POLO

116 SHOW JUMPING AND EVENTING

WHEELS AND MOTORS

120 FORMULA 1 AND INDYCAR

122 RALLYING

124 MOTORCYCLES

126 DRAG RACING

128 CYCLING

130 MOUNTAIN BIKING AND BMX

132 SKATEBOARDING

134 POWER ON

EXTREME SPORTS

138 FREE DIVING AND CLIFF DIVING

140 SKYDIVING

142 FREERIDE MOUNTAIN BIKING AND ULTRA-RUNNING

144 EXTRA EXTREME

OLYMPIC GAMES

148 OLYMPIC HISTORY

150 SUMMER OLYMPICS

152 WINTER OLYMPICS

154 PARALYMPIC GAMES

156 GLOSSARY

158 INDEX

160 ACKNOWLEDGEMENTS

A sport for everyone

Sports have been played and enjoyed for thousands of years. Today, there are hundreds of different sports out there, each with its own challenges and appeal.

A sport can be a test of speed and power, accuracy and precision, or control and creativity. Whatever the sporting challenge, athletes aren't born with the skills they need to succeed. They must learn the techniques that will give them that winning edge. It's all about dedication, commitment, and hours of practice.

A sport can be a personal quest, or a partnership between competitors (or even with an animal or machine). It can also bring players together, with everyone playing his or her role in the pursuit of a team victory.

Winning a gold medal at the Olympics, or lifting a World Cup trophy is a very special moment in any sportsperson's life. But sports aren't just about the winner. They promote fair play, healthy competition, and personal fitness. Millions of everyday people, like you, play and watch sports because they are fun!

All great sportspeople started where you are now. They made a decision to play. No matter your age, size, or skill, there is a sport for you. We hope this book will inspire you to take up a sport that you will enjoy and love.

Team sports

Every sportsperson needs a variety of individual skills, but in team sports the most important skill is to work well with others. Players need to coordinate with their teammates to master the art of defense, learn to pass and move, and get ready to attack and score those points and goals needed to win.

Soccer

Soccer, also known as association football, is often called the "beautiful game" and is one of the most popular sports on the planet. Whether it is played on a street corner or in front of thousands of fans, the sport combines speed, strength, and skill to produce an exciting spectacle.

Toes and heads

Players use their feet to play short, accurate passes, tackle an opponent, or blast a powerful shot at the goal. Players are allowed to use other parts of the body to control the ball, except for their arms and hands. When the ball is in the air, players can use their heads to clear a high cross, or leap full-length to score with a spectacular diving header.

A German player (in white) jumps high above a Nigerian opponent to head the ball away.

The essentials

Opposing teams wear uniforms of different colors so that the other players, referee, and fans can tell them apart. Players must wear protective shin pads. Goalkeepers wear a different-colored jersey so the referee can spot them in a crowded penalty area.

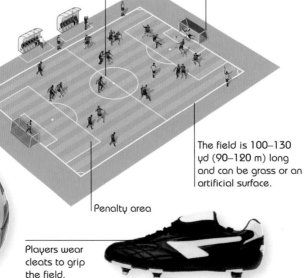

The halfway line divides the field into two halves.

The goal is 24 ft (7.32 m) wide and 8 ft (2.44 m) tall.

The field is 100–130 yd (90–120 m) long and can be grass or an artificial surface.

Penalty area

A professional ball measures 28 in (70 cm) in circumference.

Players wear cleats to grip the field.

A player from the Brazilian national team (in yellow) challenges a player from Portugal during a World Cup match.

 Soccer is played by two teams of 11 players.

Teams try to move a ball up the field to score goals. At the same time, they will also try to stop the opposition from scoring.

A goal is scored when the ball crosses the goal line between the two goal posts and under the crossbar.

Each match lasts a minimum of 90 minutes, which is split into two halves of 45 minutes.

In some soccer competitions, extra time is played if the score is level at the end of the game. If the scores are still level at the end of extra time, teams take part in a penalty shootout.

Soccer matches are overseen by a referee. The referee can warn players for serious fouls by showing a yellow card, or send players off the field for very bad offenses by showing a red card.

Attackers must keep two or more opposition players between themselves and the goal before the ball is passed to them. If this does not happen, then the attacking player is offside and the defending team is awarded a free kick.

World's best

The top tournament for national soccer teams is the World Cup, which is held every four years. Each country also has its own domestic league and cup competitions. Soccer is also played in different forms, as well as the 11-a-side game. These include indoor games, such as five-a-side and Futsal, and even beach soccer, which is played on a sand field.

Goalkeepers wear gloves to help them catch the ball. They can only handle the ball inside their own penalty area.

Playing as a team

A soccer team is split into four different position groups: the goalkeeper, defenders, midfielders, and forwards. Each team has just one goalkeeper on the field at one time. Defenders help the goalkeeper to protect their own goal and stop the opposition from scoring. Midfielders play in the middle of the field and help out the defenders. They also link up with the forwards, who look to create and score goals. A professional team can make up to three substitutions a match.

Baseball

Since its earliest mention in the middle of the 18th century, baseball has grown to become America's national sport. Today, millions of fans follow the action and news from leagues throughout North and Central America and Asia.

Baseball is played by two teams. Each team is made up of nine players.

A game consists of nine innings. Each inning sees both teams bat and field.

Teams swap between batting and fielding when the fielding team gets three batters out.

Teams score runs when a batter runs around all four bases.

A "strike" occurs when a pitch flies through the strike zone. It also occurs when a pitch is hit and travels outside the foul lines or if a batter swings and misses a pitch.

Batters can be "out" in a number of ways. A "strikeout" sees a batter make three strikes. A "flyout" sees the batter hit the ball, which is then caught by a fielder. A "tagout" sees a fielder with the ball touch a batter running between bases. Batters are also "out" if they don't reach a base before the ball is thrown to the fielder standing there.

The pitcher throws the ball from a mound that is 60 ft 6 in (16.4 m) in front of the batter.

Pitching the ball

The pitcher throws, or pitches, the ball at the batter. A pitcher can choose from a number of different types of pitch. The "fastball" is a fast, direct pitch. The "changeup" is slower than a fastball, while the "curveball" dips before it reaches the batter. The "slider" is a type of pitch that moves sideways in the air after it has been thrown.

Fastballs can travel at 100 mph (160 kph).

The essentials

The three bases and home plate are arranged in a diamond shape. The ball is made out of rubber or cork that is wrapped in yarn and covered with leather. The baseball bat is made from wood or metal.

The outfield fence marks the edge of the playing area.

The batter stands over home plate with the catcher behind.

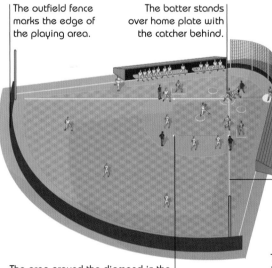

The glove has a padded palm and webbing between the fingers.

The foul lines mark the sides of the playing area.

The area around the diamond is the infield. Beyond this is the outfield.

The ball measures 3 in (7.5 cm) across.

Bats are no more than 42 in (106.7 cm) long.

Batter up

Batters will try to score as many runs as possible. The most spectacular way to do this is by hitting a home run. This is when in a single hit, the batter runs around all the bases unchallenged. A home run usually happens when the batter hits the ball beyond the outfield fence. Batters must run if they hit the ball into the playing area. They have to reach a base before the fielders throw the ball there. Batters will then try to run to the other bases while their teammates bat.

Helmets protect the batter against the hard ball.

Fielders wear a large, padded glove on their non-throwing hand to stop or catch the ball.

In the field

The goal of the fielding side is to get three batters out and to restrict any run-scoring chances. In addition to the pitcher, the fielding side has seven fielders. Four of these stand in the infield, usually close to the bases, and three in the outfield. The final member of the fielding side is the catcher, who wears an extra-thick glove to catch pitches.

Batters usually wear gloves so that the bat does not slip in their hands.

The batter stands inside a small box marked on the floor to one side of the home plate.

Jargon buster

Double play: when the fielding side gets two batters out during the same passage of play.

Foul ball: when a ball hit by a batter travels outside the foul lines.

Stealing a base: when a batter manages to run to the next base while the pitcher is trying to pitch the ball.

Strike zone: the area over home plate between the batter's knees and a point halfway between the shoulder and the belt.

13

Basketball

Fast, furious, and physical, basketball is a breathtaking sport where players shoot a ball at high hoops to score points. It is played in many countries around the world, and is very popular in the United States.

Aim of the game

A basketball team has 12 players, with five on the court at any one time and seven substitutes. Players can be swapped at any time with any of the substitutes.

Points are scored when the ball goes down through a hoop at either end of the court. Behind the hoop is a large backboard.

Each game has four periods, which last for 10 minutes. If the scores are level at the end of the 40 minutes, an overtime of 5 minutes is played.

When a team gets the ball, it has 24 seconds to score. If it doesn't score, the ball is given to the opposition.

Once the ball is in the attacking half, it cannot be passed back over the halfway line.

Players must dribble the ball as they run down the court. This involves bouncing the ball with one hand.

If players do not bounce the ball while moving, then they will be penalized for "traveling."

If a player bounces the ball, catches it with two hands, and then starts to bounce it again, the referee will penalize him or her for a "double dribble" and give the ball to the opposition.

Passing and dribbling

Players move the ball around the court by throwing or passing it to a teammate. The most common pass is the chest pass, but others include the overhead pass and the bounce pass. Players can also bounce, or dribble, the ball as they run down the court.

A player must always keep his or her dribbling hand above the ball. Otherwise they will be penalized for a "carry."

The essentials

Basketball players wear loose-fitting clothing so they can move around easily. They wear special shoes with ankle supports that protect the players as they jump and land. A basketball is filled with air so it bounces high off the hard, court floor. A ball is usually covered with small dimples to make it easy to grip.

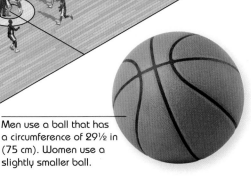

The end of the court that a team attacks is called the front court.

The basket is 10 ft (3.05 m) from the ground.

Three-point arc

The end of the court that a team defends is called the back court.

The free-throw line is 15 ft (4.6 m) in front of the backboard.

Men use a ball that has a circumference of 29½ in (75 cm). Women use a slightly smaller ball.

Shoot and score

The number of points scored depends on where a shot is taken. Three points are awarded to a team if a player scores a basket from outside the three-point arc. A basket scored from inside the three-point arc is worth two points. If a foul is committed by a player then the opposition may be awarded free throws. These are unopposed shots taken from the free-throw line and score one point.

Players can bounce the ball off the backboard to help score baskets.

The hoop measures 17¾ in (45 cm) in diameter.

A player from the Memphis Grizzlies (in white) jumps high to score a slam dunk.

Hoop dreams

Teams will try to get the ball close to the hoop to make scoring as easy as possible. Once under the hoop, players have a couple of choices. They can score with a lay-up, where they jump up and bounce the ball off the backboard into the hoop. More spectacular is the slam dunk where players leap high and seem to hang in the air, before pushing the ball down directly through the hoop.

Volleyball

Volleyball is an amazingly popular sport that is played in nearly every country on the planet. It can be played outdoors, indoors, and even on the beach!

Aim of the game

There are six players in a standard volleyball team.

Teams try to score points by hitting a ball over a net so it bounces in the other team's half of the court, or the other team cannot return it.

Players who cross the center line lose a point.

The first team to score 25 points wins a set, except in the last set, where the first to 15 points wins. Teams can only win a set by two clear points.

A volleyball match is made up of five sets.

After each point won, players move around the court in a clockwise direction. This means that all players have a chance to serve and play in every position.

The ball weighs between 9–10 oz (260–280 g) and is 8½ in (22 cm) in diameter.

On the court

While matches can be played on many surfaces, professional courts are made of wood or artificial materials. Lines on the court show where players should stand at the start of each point. The attack line is behind the center line and a team's attackers stand in front of it. The area behind the attack line is called the back zone. This is where the defenders stand.

The net height is 7 ft 11 in (2.43 m) for men and 7 ft 4 in (2.24 m) for women.

Attack line

The court is 60 ft (18 m) long and 29 ft (9 m) wide.

Over the net

After a serve, teams have up to three touches to get the ball back over the net. They can use any body part, as long as they do not catch or carry the ball.

On the beach

An Olympic sport since 1996, beach volleyball is played on a smaller court of sand. There are just two players in each team and a softer, smaller ball is used.

The two players have to work very hard to defend their half of the court.

Netball

Netball is a fast-paced sport that was developed from basketball. It sees players run, leap, pass, and catch a ball to outsmart the opposition and score points.

Aim of the game

There are seven players on a netball team.

A netball match is divided into four 15-minute periods.

One point is scored every time the ball goes down through a netted hoop on a goalpost.

When a player catches the ball, the first foot he or she puts down is called the landing foot. The player cannot take another step with this foot until the ball has been passed.

A player has three seconds to pass the ball after catching it.

Penalties are awarded if players obstruct, or make contact with their opponents, and for other discipline issues. The offending player must leave the court until the ball has left the penalty-taker's hands.

Scoring points

A game of netball starts in the center circle, with one player passing the ball to a teammate. Players must move the ball down the court to get it to the goal circle, while defenders try to stop them. Attacking players then try to shoot the ball through the hoop to score a point.

The court is divided into thirds, with shooting circles at each end and a center circle in the middle.

A 10-ft (3.05-m) high goalpost is in the middle of the shooting circle.

A netball court is 100 ft (30.5 m) long and 50 ft (15.25 m) wide.

Moving around

Players wear initials to show their playing positions. The positions are Goal Shooter (GS), Goal Attack (GA), Wing Attack (WA), Center (C), Wing Defense (WD), Goal Defense (GD), and Goalkeeper (GK). Their positions determine where players are allowed to go on the court. The Center can move in any area, except the two shooting circles. The Goal Shooter can move in the attacking third and the shooting circle.

Football

Football is a fast and aggressive full-contact contest where two teams try to pass, carry, and force the ball toward their opponents' end zone. Each team is divided into three units: offense, defense, and special teams.

The offense

The quarterback, wide receivers, offensive linemen, and running backs form the offense of a football team. Their role is to gain territory and score points. They have a series of four attempts, called downs, to move the ball at least 10 yards (9.1 m) toward the defense's end zone. If successful, they are awarded another four downs. This continues until they score, run out of time, or the ball is given to the opposition.

This offensive lineman is blocking the defense from getting to his quarterback.

The quarterback usually leads the offense and decides what plays to make.

Defensive positions include the linemen, linebackers, cornerbacks, and the safeties.

The defense

The defense's main goal is to stop the opposition offense from scoring by tackling players who have the ball. They also try to gain possession for their team. They do this by breaking up plays and intercepting passes. They can also tackle, or "sack," the opposition quarterback.

Special teams

Special teams are involved in specialized moves during the game. These include kicking field goals and extra points, punting the ball to the opposition, and returning kicks. In addition to kickers, the special team is made up of snappers, ball holders, and kick returners. Snappers restart play by passing the ball back through their legs to a teammate, while ball holders keep the ball upright when a field goal or extra point is taken. The returners catch kickoffs and punts, and then carry the ball back up the field.

The ball holder places the ball and holds it upright so that the kicker can hit the ball cleanly.

Even though each team may have 40–50 players, there are only 11 players from each team on the field at the same time.

A game is divided up into four quarters, each of which lasts 15 minutes. Teams swap ends for each quarter.

Points are scored by catching or carrying the ball into the opposition's end zone. This is called a touchdown and it is worth six points.

After a touchdown, the offense can score an extra point by kicking the ball through the goalposts, or two points by running and passing the ball into the end zone.

Field goals are worth three points. They are scored by kicking the ball through the opposition's goalposts.

Defenses can score points for their own team. If they tackle an opponent in his own end zone, then they will be awarded a safety, which scores two points.

Penalties are given when the rules are broken. Players are not allowed to push an opponent in the back, hold a player other than the ball carrier, or illegally obstruct a player.

The essentials

Football is a full-contact sport and so each part of a player's body needs to be protected. The field is 100 yards (91 m) long with an end zone at either end. The yards are marked on the field to show how far the teams have to move the ball.

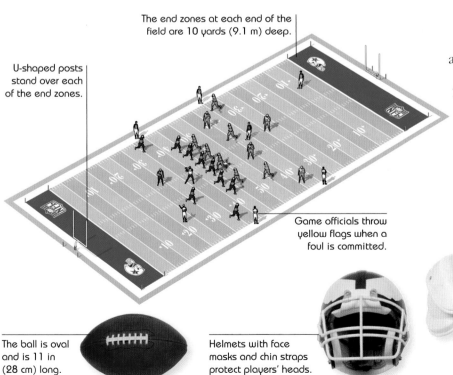

The end zones at each end of the field are 10 yards (9.1 m) deep.

U-shaped posts stand over each of the end zones.

Game officials throw yellow flags when a foul is committed.

Shoulder pads protect the shoulders, chest, and upper back.

The ball is oval and is 11 in (28 cm) long.

Helmets with face masks and chin straps protect players' heads.

19

Rugby union

Rugby is an action-packed contact sport. There are several different types of rugby, including rugby league and rugby sevens, but rugby union is the most popular form. Every four years, teams from nearly 100 countries try to qualify for the rugby World Cup.

The player mus[t] place the ba[ll] down over the tr[y] line to score a try.

Scoring points

There are four ways to score points: tries, conversions, penalty kicks, and dro[p] goals. A try, which is worth five points, can be converted with a place kick known as a conversion. This is worth two points. Successful penalty kick[s] and drop goals are worth three points.

Aim of the game

Rugby union teams are made up of 15 players.

A rugby game is made up of two halves of 40 minutes each.

Players can throw and catch, or kick the ball to move it up the field toward the opposition's try line, where players can score tries.

Passes must always be sideways or backward. A forward pass will see a scrum being given to the opposition.

The opposition will try to stop attacking moves by tackling the player with the ball.

Only the player with the ball can be tackled. Tackles cannot be made above the shoulders. Illegal tackles will result in a penalty to the opposing team.

If the ball crosses the touchline, the game is restarted with a lineout where the ball went out.

Players shown a yellow card for breaking a law are "sin-binned" and must leave the field for 10 minutes. For serious offences, the referee will show a red card, and the player has to leave the field for the rest of the match.

Move the ball

Players try to move the ball up the field by running with it, kicking it, or passing it backward or sideways to a teammate. At the same time, the defending players will try to stop any attackers with the ball by grabbing hold of them and tackling them. Play does not stop once a tackle has been made, and teams will compete for the ball in special team moves called rucks and mauls.

Fields are no longer than 110 yards (100 m) from one try line to the other.

The try line marks the start of the in-goal area.

In-goal area

The crossbar of the posts is 10 ft (3 m) above the ground.

Cleats should not have any sharp edges on them.

A rugby ball measures 11–12 in (28–30 cm) long.

The essentials

In the center of each try line are the H-shaped posts. Successful kicks must travel over the horizontal crossbar and between the uprights. Rugby players wear jerseys, shorts, and shoes with cleats on them. Some players wear shoulder padding, mouth guards, and padded headgear for extra protection.

Two players from Ireland (in green) try to tackle an attacking player from South Africa.

Scrums see both sets of forwards join together and try to push each other off the ball.

Backs and forwards

The 15 players on a rugby union team are split up into two groups: forwards and backs. The forwards wear numbers one to eight. They are usually involved in restarts after the referee has stopped the game. These include scrums and lineouts. The backs wear numbers nine to 15. They are usually involved in attacking moves once the ball has been passed away from a restart, and in defending against opposition attacks.

Jargon buster

Maul: a passage of play after a tackle when players compete for the ball if the tackled player has stayed on his or her feet.

Ruck: a passage of play after a tackle when players compete for the ball after the tackled player has been brought to the ground.

Knock-on: when a player drops or pushes the ball forward. The referee will stop play and award a scrum to the opposition.

Lineout: a way of restarting a game after the ball has gone out of play. Two groups of forwards line up against each other while another player throws the ball into play for them to catch.

21

Australian rules

Australian rules football began as a way to keep cricket players in shape during the winter months. Today, it is a fast-paced contact sport where two teams tackle and obstruct each other to prevent goals from being scored.

A pack of players competes to catch the ball.

Aim of the game

Australian rules is played by two teams of 18 players. There are also four interchange players who sit on the bench.

A game lasts 80 minutes plus time added on.

The team that scores the most points wins the game.

Points are scored by passing or kicking the ball through the opposition's set of goal posts.

If the ball is kicked between the two tall goal posts, the attacking team scores a goal, which is worth six points.

If the ball travels between a goal post and a smaller "behind post" to one side, then a behind, worth one point, is scored.

If a defending player touches the ball before it goes between any of the posts, it is called a behind and only worth one point.

Players are allowed to kick, slap, and carry the ball, but they are not allowed to throw it.

Players running with the ball must bounce it every 50 ft (15 m)—otherwise they will be penalized.

Team profile

There are no set positions in Australian rules football and players can move freely around the field. However, teams are usually made up of six forwards, six defenders, and six midfielders. The forwards, responsible for attacking moves, are often the goal scorers. The defenders, or backmen, try to stop the opposition from scoring goals by obstructing and tackling them. The midfielders are the link between the forwards and the backmen.

No throwing

To get the ball into a good scoring position, players try to move it closer to the opposition goal posts. Players are not allowed to throw the ball to each other. Instead, it is kicked, slapped, and punched from teammate to teammate as they run.

Players use handpasses to make short passes to teammates.

The posts

A set of four posts sits at each end of the Australian rules field. The two tall central posts are the goal posts. On each side of these are the smaller behind posts. The base of each post is usually covered with thick padding so that players are not hurt if they run into them. Standing behind each set of posts is the goal umpire, who signals whether a goal or a behind has been scored.

In front of the two goal posts is the goal square, which is 30 ft (9 m) wide.

At restarts, four players from each team are allowed in the center square.

Goal post

Behind post

The oval is 443–607 ft (135–185 m) long.

An Australian rules ball is oval in shape.

The essentials

Australian rules was originally played on cricket fields, which varied in size. Today, some teams have their own specially built stadiums. Players need little equipment—although this is a contact sport, they do not wear protective padding or headgear. Their uniform is made up of a jersey (called a guernsey), shorts, socks, and shoes with cleats for extra grip.

Ice hockey

Players are allowed to body check each other during a game of ice hockey, making it one of the roughest, but most exciting, team sports to watch and play.

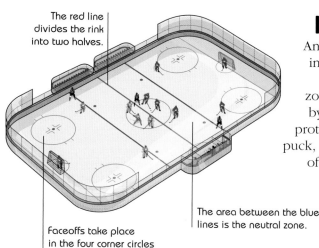

The red line divides the rink into two halves.

Faceoffs take place in the four corner circles and the center circle.

The area between the blue lines is the neutral zone.

Ice protection

An ice hockey rink is divided into thirds, with goalposts at each end in the attacking zone. The rink is surrounded by tall Plexiglass boards that protect the spectators from the puck, which can travel at speeds of up to 120 mph (190 kph).

Aim of the game

There are up to 22 players on an ice hockey team, with six players on the ice at a time.

Players use sticks to hit the puck across the ice to score goals.

A game of ice hockey is divided into three 20-minute periods.

To start the game and to restart it after a goal is scored, players take part in a faceoff. Here, two players square up to each other while the referee drops the puck between them.

Players must follow the puck into the attacking zone, otherwise they will be offside.

When players hit the puck over the halfway line and across the red line level with a goal, they are guilty of "icing," and play is restarted with a faceoff.

The puck is made from rubber.

Sticks are 6 ft 6 in (2 m) long.

Players wear hockey skates.

On the ice

An ice-hockey team has six players on the ice rink at one time. There are three main positions—goaltender, defense, and attack. The goaltender and two defensemen protect the goal and try to stop the opposition from scoring. The three attackers, known as forwards, try to create and score goals. Players clash and tackle as they compete for the puck, but only the player with the puck is allowed to be shoved or pushed, which is called a body check.

Protective padding, including body armor, gloves, and helmets, is an essential part of a hockey player's gear.

Field hockey

Hockey is a team sport that has been played in various forms for thousands of years. Today, it is played indoors and outdoors in more than 120 countries.

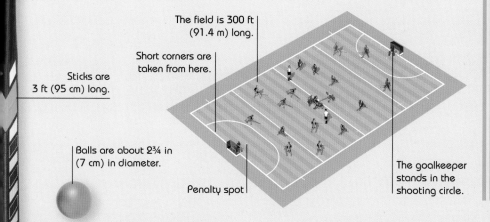

The field is 300 ft (91.4 m) long.

Short corners are taken from here.

Sticks are 3 ft (95 cm) long.

Balls are about 2¾ in (7 cm) in diameter.

Penalty spot

The goalkeeper stands in the shooting circle.

Aim of the game

The 11 players on a team hit, push, and pass a ball with sticks to score goals.

Goals can be scored only from inside the opponent's shooting circle, when the ball crosses the opponent's line between the goal posts. The team with the most goals at the end of the match wins.

A match lasts 70 minutes and is split into two halves of 35 minutes each.

Only the goalkeeper can use his or her feet to stop the ball.

If an opposition player commits a foul around the goal area, then a short corner is awarded. Here, a free hit is taken from a mark inside the shooting circle.

Fouls in the shooting circle result in a penalty stroke, where one player shoots at the goal from the penalty spot with only the goalkeeper to beat.

Sticks and fields

The crook-shaped end of a hockey stick is flat on the one side and rounded on the other. Players must use the flat side of the stick to hit the ball. Traditionally, hockey was played on a grass field. Today, however, it is also played on an artificial surface, which allows the ball to travel at great speeds around the field.

Attack and defense

A hockey team is made up of attackers and defenders. Attackers include the wingers, inside forwards, and center forwards. Their job is to move the ball up the field to score goals. The opposition's defense will try to stop them. Defenders include the fullbacks, half backs, and the goalkeeper. Players are not allowed to make contact with their opponents. If they do, they are penalized by the referee.

A field hockey goal is 12 ft (3.7 m) wide and 7 ft (2.1 m) high.

The goalkeeper wears protective clothing, including a face mask and chest pads.

Cricket

Cricket is a bat-and-ball game of technique and concentration. One team bats to score runs (points), while their opponent tries to "bowl them out." They then swap and the roles are reversed.

The essentials

Cricket is played on an oval-shaped ground with a field in the middle. At each end of the field, called the pitch, are wickets, each made up of three stumps with two small pieces of wood, called bails, on top. The cricket ball is made from cork and string and covered with red or white leather. It has a large seam running around its middle. Bats can vary in size and weight but can not be larger than 38 in (97 cm) long and 4¼ in (10.8 cm) wide.

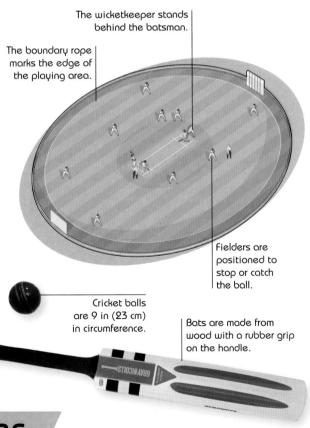

The wicketkeeper stands behind the batsman.

The boundary rope marks the edge of the playing area.

Fielders are positioned to stop or catch the ball.

Cricket balls are 9 in (23 cm) in circumference.

Bats are made from wood with a rubber grip on the handle.

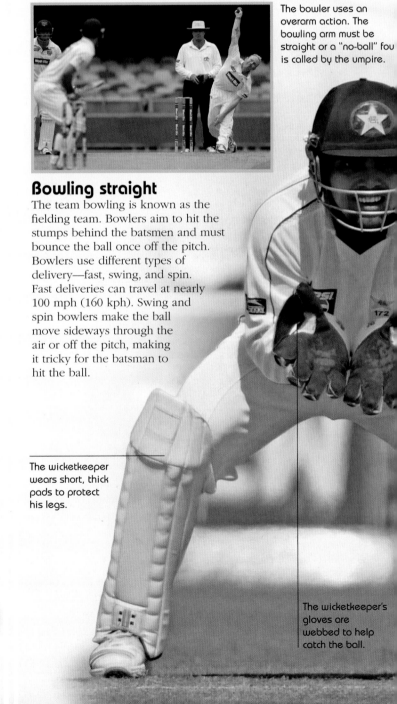

The bowler uses an overarm action. The bowling arm must be straight or a "no-ball" fou is called by the umpire.

Bowling straight

The team bowling is known as the fielding team. Bowlers aim to hit the stumps behind the batsmen and must bounce the ball once off the pitch. Bowlers use different types of delivery—fast, swing, and spin. Fast deliveries can travel at nearly 100 mph (160 kph). Swing and spin bowlers make the ball move sideways through the air or off the pitch, making it tricky for the batsman to hit the ball.

The wicketkeeper wears short, thick pads to protect his legs.

The wicketkeeper's gloves are webbed to help catch the ball.

At the crease

Two players from the batting team are on the pitch at one time. One batsman faces the bowler's delivery and the other batsman stands at the opposite end of the pitch. To score one run the facing batsman needs to hit the ball and run from wicket to wicket (swapping with the other batsman), before the fielding team collects and throws the ball at the stumps. A batsman scores four runs by hitting the ball over the boundary rope. If a batsman hits the ball over the boundary rope without the ball bouncing, he scores six runs.

If the batsman hits the ball and a fielder catches it without it bouncing, the batsman is out.

If the ball hits the sweetspot of the bat it will go farther and faster.

In the field

The fielding team needs to get 10 batsmen "out" to end the innings. Batsmen are out in a number of ways. If a bowler's delivery hits the stumps, the batsman is "bowled out." A batsman can be out "leg-before-wicket" (LBW), when a delivery hits his pads when it would have gone on to hit the stumps. A batsman can also be caught after hitting the ball, or "run out" if the fielding team gets the ball to the stumps before the batsmen finish their run.

Helmets are fitted with metal faceguards.

Padded gloves protect hands.

The stumps are 28 in (71 cm) high.

Aim of the game

● A cricket match is played between two teams of 11 players.

Each team is given a chance to score runs by batting. The team that scores the most runs wins the game.

All players on a team must bat, but only specialized bowlers bowl. Each team also has a fielder, called a wicketkeeper.

The bowler bowls the ball to the batsman, who must then hit it to score runs.

A bowler bowls a set of six deliveries. This is called an over. At the end of an over, another bowler takes a turn and bowls from the other end of the pitch.

A run is scored when a batsman hits the ball and successfully runs to the stumps at the other end of the pitch.

In a limited-overs game, each team has a set number of overs (usually 20 or 50) to score more runs than the opposition.

In a timed game, teams have a set amount of time to bat and bowl. The team that scores the most runs must also get the other team "all out" in the set time to win.

Other teams

Being part of a team is a good way to make friends and allows you to learn from others. If you haven't found your favorite team sport yet, there are many more to choose from. Why not try one of these?

Hurling

Two teams of 15 players hit a small ball with sticks, called hurleys. The goal is to score points by hitting the ball over the crossbar of the opposition's goal (one point) or into the goal (three points).

Ultimate

In this non-contact sport two teams of seven players throw a flying disk around a playing area and aim to score points by getting a teammate to catch the disk in the opposition's end zone.

Softball

Softball is similar to its parent sport baseball. The main differences are the softball diamond is smaller, the pitcher throws the ball underarm, and the ball is larger and less dense than a normal baseball.

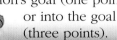

Handball

Handball is a high-scoring sport where two teams of seven players use their hands to pass a ball around a field. The goal is to throw the ball into the opposition's goal.

Sepak takraw

Players use their feet, hands, knees, and chest to get the ball over a net 5 ft (1.5 m) high. They score points if the opposition cannot return the ball.

Futsal

This is a five-a-side version of soccer. It uses a heavier ball than normal soccer and the ball doesn't bounce as high, so players must concentrate on control and making short passes.

29

Racket sports

Racket sports are a mix of power, speed, and technique. Players need excellent hand-eye coordination to follow and strike fast-moving balls and birdies, in addition to a delicate touch to outwit their opponents. Players also need high levels of concentration, determination, and stamina to cope with the long matches and important match-winning moments.

Tennis

Tennis is played on a variety of surfaces, including clay, concrete, and grass. Tennis players need to be fast to reach all parts of the court. Top players combine speed with great coordination and a variety of shots to defeat their opponents.

Rackets are allowed to be up to 29 in (73.6 cm) long.

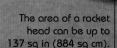

The area of a racket head can be up to 137 sq in (884 sq cm).

A range of shots

Tennis shots can be played with the forehand (on the same side as the hand holding the racket), or the backhand (on the side opposite the hand holding the racket). Many tennis players use two hands to play the backhand for extra power. A player can allow the ball to bounce once before playing a shot. They can also hit the ball before it bounces. This is called a volley. Hitting a volley when the ball is above head height is called a smash.

Serving

Each point starts with a serve. The server must stand behind the baseline at the back of the court and hit the ball cleanly over the net so that it bounces in the service box diagonally opposite. If the player fails to serve correctly, a "fault" is called and they serve again. If the server faults with their second serve, the point is awarded to the opponent.

Tennis shoes have wide, flat soles to improve grip and stability on the court.

Singles and doubles

Many tennis matches involve one player against another. These are known as singles matches. Tennis matches can also involve two players on each side. These are called doubles matches, and are played using the full width of the tennis court. In doubles matches, the serve rotates after each game so that each player gets to serve in turn.

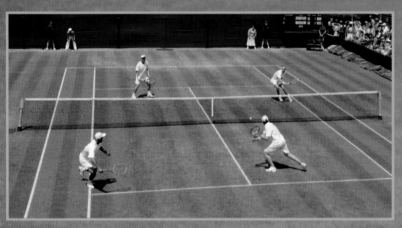

To keep from colliding or going for the same shot, doubles players need to communicate with their partners.

Tennis players aim to score points to win games and sets.

A point is scored when one of the players fails to return the ball to their opponent's side of the court. If a player lets the ball bounce more than once, hits the ball into the net, or hits the ball so that its first bounce is outside the court, the point is awarded to the opponent.

One player serves for all the points throughout each game. A player must reach at least four points and have two more points than their opponent to win a game. In the next game, the other player serves.

Zero points is called "love"; one point is called "15"; two points is called "30"; three points is called "40." When the score reaches 40–40, this is known as "deuce."

The first player to win 6 games, wins the set, but each set must be won by 2 clear games, such as 6 games to 4. A tie-break is played when the games score reaches 6–6.

The first player to win two sets wins the match. Some men's competitions have longer matches, where players must win three sets.

The essentials

The most important part of any tennis player's gear is the racket. The tightness of the strings can be altered to suit a player's style—looser strings give more power, while tighter strings give more control. The tennis ball is yellow or white to help players see it more easily.

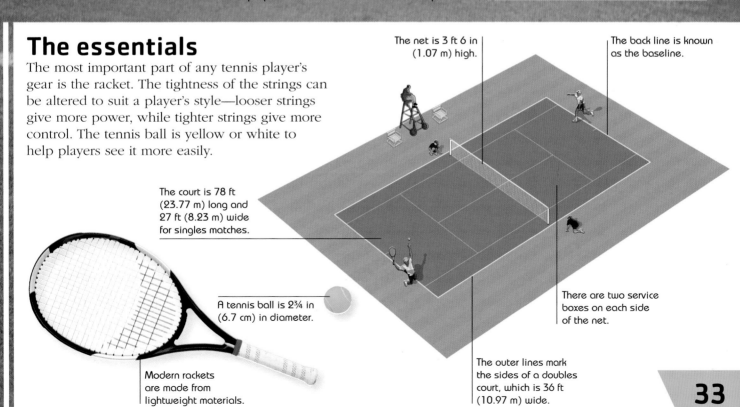

The net is 3 ft 6 in (1.07 m) high.

The back line is known as the baseline.

The court is 78 ft (23.77 m) long and 27 ft (8.23 m) wide for singles matches.

A tennis ball is 2¾ in (6.7 cm) in diameter.

There are two service boxes on each side of the net.

Modern rackets are made from lightweight materials.

The outer lines mark the sides of a doubles court, which is 36 ft (10.97 m) wide.

33

Table tennis

Also known as ping-pong, table tennis is a fast-paced indoor racket game. Players will try to smash and spin the ball to trick opponents and win points.

Aim of the game

Table tennis matches are won by the first player to win three or five games.

A game is won when a player scores 11 points. If the scores are 10–10, play continues until one player is two points clear of the other.

A point is scored when the ball bounces twice on the opponent's side of the table or bounces once then hits the floor. However, hitting the ball before it bounces, called volleying, is not allowed.

A point is awarded to an opponent if a player hits the ball twice, hits it with anything other than the paddle, returns the ball so that it bounces on his or her side of the net, or places his or her hand on the table.

After-dinner games

Table tennis has not always been a game of speed and fierce competition. It was originally played in the 19th century as an after-dinner game. People would set up the dining-room table with books for the net. A round champagne cork was then hit across the table using cigar box lids.

The table is 5 ft (1.53 m) wide and 9 ft (2.74 m) long. The net is 6 in (15.3 cm) high.

By flicking their wrists, players can spin the ball to trick an opponent.

When served, the ball must go across the center line in the opponent's half.

Paddle surfaces

Paddles are also known as bats. They are usually made from wood and can be any size, weight, or shape. Large paddles are hard to use so most are around 6 in (15 cm) wide and 10 in (25 cm) high. Each side of the paddle can be covered in a different type of rubber to suit the player's game. Some rubbers create more spin. One side of the paddle must always be red and the other side must be black.

One side of the paddle may be dimpled to increase any spin.

The ball measures 1¼ in (4 cm) across and weighs 0.1 oz (2.7 g).

Badminton

With a highest recorded birdie speed of more than 185 mph (300 kph), badminton is one of the quickest and most exciting racket sports to play and watch.

The birdie

Badminton is different from other racket sports because badminton players hit a birdie over the net. A birdie weighs just 0.25 oz (5 g). Its weight and shape allow it to travel at great speeds. But it is also very delicate—professional players may need to change birdies after each point.

The birdie has a feathered tail to help its flight.

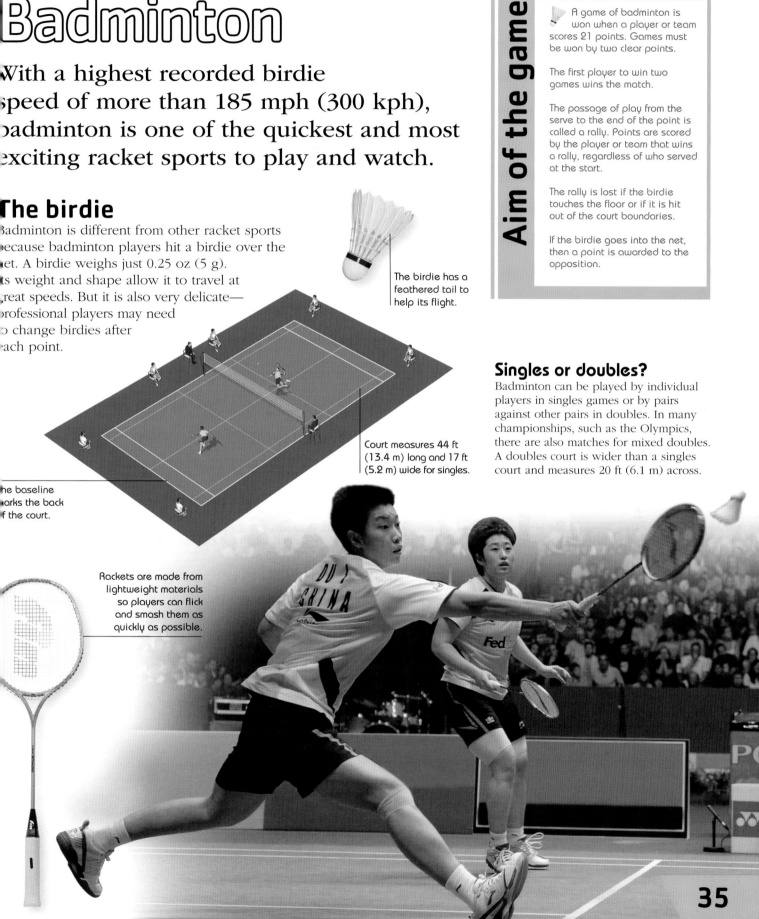

Court measures 44 ft (13.4 m) long and 17 ft (5.2 m) wide for singles.

The baseline marks the back of the court.

Rackets are made from lightweight materials so players can flick and smash them as quickly as possible.

Aim of the game

A game of badminton is won when a player or team scores 21 points. Games must be won by two clear points.

The first player to win two games wins the match.

The passage of play from the serve to the end of the point is called a rally. Points are scored by the player or team that wins a rally, regardless of who served at the start.

The rally is lost if the birdie touches the floor or if it is hit out of the court boundaries.

If the birdie goes into the net, then a point is awarded to the opposition.

Singles or doubles?

Badminton can be played by individual players in singles games or by pairs against other pairs in doubles. In many championships, such as the Olympics, there are also matches for mixed doubles. A doubles court is wider than a singles court and measures 20 ft (6.1 m) across.

The strung area of a racket can be no more than 90 sq in (500 cm²).

Squash

This fast-paced and physically exhausting sport was developed more than 140 years ago. Today, there are about 50,000 squash courts in 185 countries around the world.

Part of the serving player's foot must stay in the service box.

Shoes should be non-marking and cannot have black soles.

Serving

Squash games are played for points. Each point begins with a serve. The serving player must hit the ball without it bouncing. The ball has to hit the front wall between the service line (halfway up the front wall) and the out line (which runs around the top of the whole court). It then needs to bounce in the opponent's quarter of the court.

The name of the game

Squash gets its name from the squashable rubber balls used in the game. Different types of ball are used, depending on players' abilities. The ball used by beginners is hard and bounces high, making it easier to hit. Professionals use a softer ball that has a low bounce.

Squash is played in an enclosed court by two or four players.

Players hit the ball against a front wall to score points. The ball can come off the side walls and the back wall, as long as it hits the front wall and stays below the out line and above the tin, which runs along the bottom of the front wall.

A point is scored if an opponent fails to return the ball before it bounces twice. If the ball goes above the out line or below the tin, a point or the service is awarded to the opposing player.

The player who wins the point is given the serve. This player continues to serve until he or she loses a point. When this happens, the serve passes to the opponent.

If a ball hits a player before hitting the front wall, a "let" is called and the point played again.

There are two scoring systems. One sees points awarded to either player, regardless of who served. In the other system, only the serving player scores points. When he or she loses a point, the other player serves.

A game is won by the first player to reach 11 points. Players must win a match by two clear points. Each match is played to the first to win two or three games.

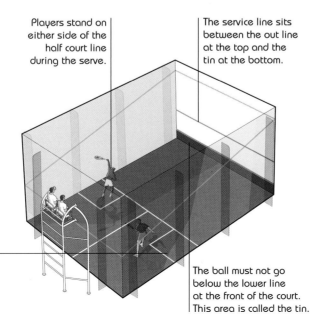

Even with a wider court, doubles players bump and jostle for space during a match.

Doubles

Squash is played by either two players or as a game of doubles. Doubles matches are played by two teams of men, two women, or a mixed pair. Doubles squash is fast and potentially dangerous as the four players chase around on a court that is the same length, but slightly wider, than a singles court.

The essentials

In addition to comfortable clothes, a squash player's gear bag includes rackets, balls, and often goggles. The maximum allowed weight of a racket is 9 oz (255 g). This is why rackets are made from lightweight materials, such as graphite, titanium, or kevlar.

Players stand on either side of the half court line during the serve.

The service line sits between the out line at the top and the tin at the bottom.

Rackets cannot be longer than 27 in (68.5 cm).

Goggles protect eyes.

A colored dot shows how soft the ball is.

The service boxes sit against either side wall.

The ball must not go below the lower line at the front of the court. This area is called the tin.

Different rackets

All racket sports test a player's concentration and coordination. Some racket sports are fast and powerful; others require good technique and precision. There are many racket sports out there for you to discover.

Jai-alai

This fast-action sport uses a curved, basket-shaped racket. The court has a front and side wall that players throw the ball at. A point is scored when the ball bounces twice after it has hit the front wall.

Soft tennis

This version of tennis is played indoors or outdoors and uses a soft rubber ball. The ball is hard to hit powerfully, so the matches have longer rallies.

Racquetball

This fast-paced sport uses a racket, ball, and court similar to squash. Players have to hit the ball against the court's front wall to try to score points. There's a lot of running, so the sport is a great way to keep fit.

Jianzi

Players pass a special shuttle, called a chapteh, over a net and gain points for each successful hit. The game is usually played on a badminton court, and can be played with or without a net.

Real tennis

This is the original version of tennis and was popular in the 16th and 17th centuries. It is played indoors on a special court with lots of markings. The ball is heavier than a lawn tennis ball and players use wooden rackets.

Pickleball

Pickleball was invented in the US. It is played on a court similar in size to a badminton court, but with a low net. To score points, players use a paddle to hit the rubber ball so their opponent can't return it.

Lacrosse

A small, hard rubber ball is thrown and carried by players using a special stick called the crosse. The stick has a net pocket on one end to hold the ball. Players pass the ball around the field and try to score goals.

Track & field and gymnastics

Athletes are pushed to the limit with running, jumping, vaulting, and throwing events. Weightlifting is the ultimate test of strength, while gymnasts show off amazing moves on apparatus and rhythmic routines on the floor.

Sprinting

True tests of speed and power, the sprints are often some of the most-watched events in a track & field competition. Sprints take place over 60, 100, 200, and 400 meters, and over hurdles.

Sprinters drive off their starting blocks, pumping their legs to gain speed.

Sensors in starting blocks detect false starts.

On your mark

The start is very important to any sprinting race. To get a good sprint start, athletes use blocks with adjustable pedals to drive forward. Once out of the blocks, sprinters will try to lift their heads and get upright as quickly as possible. This helps them to get into the best sprinting position so they can run their fastest.

Handover

Relays are team events for sprinters. In a relay, four athletes each run 100 or 400 meters. When athletes have run their section, or leg, of the race, they hand over a small stick, called a baton, to the next runner. A bad handover can ruin a race for a team.

Hurdling

While most sprints are flat races, the hurdles see athletes go over 10 hurdles, known as gates, as they run to the finish line. Men run hurdle races over 110 and 400 meters. Women's hurdle races are held over 100 and 400 meters. Hurdlers aim to keep a smooth running style so they clear the hurdles as easily as possible. They usually have a set stride pattern to ensure that they lead with the same leg over every hurdle.

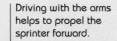

Hurdlers keep as low to the gates as possible during their race.

Driving with the arms helps to propel the sprinter forward.

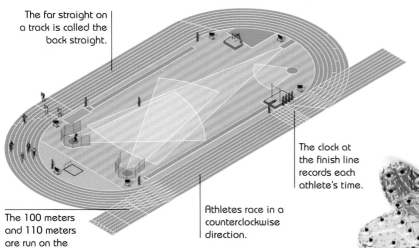

The far straight on a track is called the back straight.

The clock at the finish line records each athlete's time.

The 100 meters and 110 meters are run on the home straight.

Athletes race in a counterclockwise direction.

The essentials

An outdoor track measures 400 meters in circumference and has six or eight lanes. Athletes in the 400, 200, and 4x100 meter relay races have staggered starts, while 100-meter runners all start behind the same line. The track's surface is usually rubberized, so athletes wear shoes with spikes for maximum grip.

Spikes can be altered to suit different races.

Distance events

These running and walking races are longer than sprints and can cover great distances, testing athletes to the very limits of their endurance. They take place in an arena, around city streets, or over grueling cross-country courses.

Many marathons are run around the streets of major cities, such as Berlin.

Going the distance

The marathon is a grueling road race run over 26 miles 285 yd (42.2 km). Top athletes will run this distance in a little over two hours. Marathon running is one of the few sports where the best professional athletes can compete against thousands of amateur runners, many of whom will finish the race hours after the winners.

Fast walking

Walking events are held over distances of 20 km (12.4 miles) and 50 km (31 miles) for men, while women compete only at the shorter distance. To walk as quickly as possible, competition walkers use a stride that looks like a cross between running and walking. This is because they have to keep part of one foot on the ground at all times. Lift both feet and they will be disqualified!

Officials along the route make sure that the athletes keep part of one foot on the ground at all times.

In the arena

Inside the stadium, distance runners compete over 800, 1,500, 5,000, and 10,000 meters. Athletes in the 800 meters use a staggered start in their own lane so that they all run the same distance. To run the shortest distance possible, athletes move to the inside lanes as soon as they are allowed. Those competing in longer races start behind a single line and do not run in lanes.

Clearing jumps

Athletes run 3,000 meters during the steeplechase. They must clear 35 jumps over seven laps of the track. On each lap, there are four barriers and one water jump. The water jump is made up of a barrier in front of a pool of water. Although runners usually jump the barriers to clear them as quickly as possible, they are allowed to step on top of them.

On the water jump, runners try to leap as far from the barrier as possible, since this is where the water is shallowest.

Jumping

These events are tests of speed and power, as athletes try to jump higher or farther than anyone else. Winners are decided by the tiniest of margins, so athletes must be precise in their planning and preparation.

Long jumpers sprint to give them the speed to jump long distances. Male jumpers are moving at about 23 mph (37 kph) when they take off.

Long jump

In the long jump, athletes sprint down a runway before jumping as far as they can into a sand pit. A foul line marks the end of the runway. If any part of the athlete's foot crosses over the foul line, the jump does not count. After takeoff, athletes stretch their bodies in order to make the jump last as long as possible. They then push their arms and legs forward for landing in the pit. Athletes have three or six attempts to record their longest jump.

The foul line is sometimes marked by a line of clay that will show clearly if there has been a foul jump.

High jump

High jumpers need to clear a horizontal bar. Athletes today use a technique called the "Fosbury flop." They run up to the bar, jump up off on one foot, and then arch their bodies backward over the bar to land on the thick mat. After a successful jump, the bar is raised 1 in (2.54 cm).

Triple jumping combines speed in the runup with rhythm and power in the jump.

Hop, step, and jump

The triple jump combines a jump with a hop and a step. After a short sprint to gain speed, the athlete takes off on one foot and hops forward onto the same foot, before stepping as far as possible onto the other foot. Then he or she jumps into a sand pit. The distance jumped is measured from the takeoff board to the first mark the competitor makes in the sand.

Aim of the game

Athletes must jump as high or as far as possible. The athlete who records the farthest or highest jump wins.

If two or more pole vaulters or high jumpers have successfully jumped the same height, the winner is decided by the number of failures. The athlete with the fewest failures wins.

In high jump and pole vault, if the bar is knocked down, the jump does not count.

Officials indicate a foul jump by raising a red flag.

Pole vault

In the pole vault, athletes use a long, flexible pole to clear a high bar. Athletes can choose the height at which they start the competition. They then have three attempts to clear the bar. After a successful vault, the bar is raised and the athlete has three more attempts. If the vaulter misses three times in a row, he or she is knocked out of the competition. Very few men have cleared 19 ft 7 in (6 m), and only one woman has vaulted higher than 16 ft 5 in (5 m).

At the top of the vault, athletes push off the pole and arch their bodies over the bar.

The pole is made out of light but flexible fiberglass.

Pole vaulters land on a thick, padded mat.

Throwing

Discus, javelin, hammer, and shot put are all throwing events. Athletes who compete in these sports need to have great strength. They must be able to sprint, spin, or twist in order to throw their equipment as far as possible.

Discus

Athletes throw the discus from a circle 8 ft (2.5 m) in diameter. They have three attempts, called trials, to throw the discus as far as possible. The length of the throw is measured from the front of the circle to the point where the discus first lands.

Throwers spin around to build up speed before throwing the discus.

Javelins are 8 ft 10 in (2.7 m) long for men and 7 ft 6 in (2.3 m) for women.

Athletes use their front arm to balance themselves during a throw.

Javelin

Athletes sprint down a runway to a throwing line before hurling the javelin as far as possible. If they step over the throwing line, the throw will not count. The javelin must also come down point-first in the landing sector. Athletes have three throws to record the longest distance. The javelin also forms part of multiple sports events, such as the heptathlon for women and the decathlon for men.

Hammer

The men's hammer became an Olympic event at the 1900 Games. However, the women's hammer did not appear until the Olympics at Sydney in 2000. Athletes have three attempts to throw the hammer as far as possible. The hammer is a metal ball attached to a wire. It weighs 16 lb (7 kg) for men, and 9 lb (4 kg) for women.

Discus and hammer athletes perform their throws inside large safety cages to protect people standing nearby.

Aim of the game

Athletes in throwing events have three attempts to throw their discus, javelin, hammer, or shot as far as possible.

They must stand behind a line or within a circle to complete their throw. If the thrower steps over the line or out of the circle, their throw will not count.

At the end of their throw, athletes competing in the hammer, discus, and shot put must leave the circle through its rear half, otherwise their throw will not count. The rear half is marked by white lines on either side of the throwing circle.

In the hammer and javelin, each throw must be completed in 90 seconds.

Throws are measured from the throwing line or the front edge of the throwing circle to the landing point of the equipment.

If there is a tie, the athlete whose second-best throw was longest wins the event.

Shot put

There are two main techniques used in shot put—gliding and spinning. In the glide, the athlete faces the rear of the circle and hops to the front while twisting the hips to the front to launch the shot. The athlete's feet stay as close to the ground as possible. Some athletes spin to gain extra speed when throwing.

Shot putters rub chalk into their hands to improve their grip on the shot.

Shots weigh between 4.4 lb (2 kg) and 16 lb (7.26 kg).

Women's javelins must weigh at least 1.3 lb (600 g) and men's 1.7 lb (800 g).

The hammer wire is about 4 ft (1.2 m) long.

A men's discus weighs 4.4 lb (2 kg), and is 8¾ in (22 cm) across.

Spikes are worn for javelin.

The essentials

In addition to their throwing equipment, athletes wear special shoes. Those competing in javelin wear spiked shoes for maximum grip. Athletes in other throwing events wear smooth-soled shoes so that they can spin and glide easily in the circle.

Weightlifting

The world's strongest men and women compete in weightlifting and powerlifting. To be a successful weightlifter, you need strength, technical skill, and lots of concentration.

Men's bars weigh 20 kg (44 lb) and women's 15 kg (33 lb).

Weight disks vary from 0.25 kg (0.6 lb) to 25 kg (55 lb).

Weightlifters rub powder on their hands to help them grip the bar.

Competing classes

Weightlifters are grouped into classes according to their bodyweight, and compete against others in the same class. There are eight men's classes and seven for women. Weightlifters have three attempts to lift their target weight. The person lifting the lowest weight goes first. If their first lift is successful, the weight is increased.

Aim of the game

Weightlifters and powerlifters win by lifting the heaviest weights.

Weightlifters must hold their lift until three judges are happy it counts.

Each weightlifter has three attempts to lift a weight. If the weightlifter fails to make a successful lift, he or she is ruled out of the competition.

Weightlifters have one minute to lift a weight.

In powerlifting, if the weight is dropped to the ground after it has been lifted, then the lift does not count.

Snatch

The snatch is one of two weightlifting events. Competitors lift heavy weights that are attached to a long bar, called a barbell. They must lift the weights above their heads and hold them with locked arms for the lift to count. To begin the move, weightlifters squat down and grip the bar. They then straighten their knees, before squatting again to flip the bar over their heads. Finally, they stand up while keeping the bar over their heads.

Clean and jerk

The second weightlifting event is the clean and jerk. Weightlifters must lift the weight in two movements. The first movement is called the clean. This is when the weightlifters bring the weight onto their chest. In the second movement, the jerk, they bend their knees and straighten their arms to push the weight above their head. The weight must be held until the judges give the signal.

Using the clean and jerk technique, weightlifters can lift heavier weights than using the snatch technique.

Using the snatch technique, weightlifters can lift more than 200 kg (440 lb).

Powerlifting

Known as the strongest men and women in the world, powerlifters compete over three different categories. These are squats, deadlifts, and bench presses. Powerlifters must lift weights in all the categories and they have three attempts at each weight. The weights lifted are added together to give the powerlifter a total score.

Jargon buster

Bench press: a lift used in powerlifting where the athlete lies on a bench and lowers the weight until it touches their chest. The weight is then pushed back to its original position.

Deadlift: a powerlifting move where the barbell is lifted off the ground until the competitor is upright with a straight back.

Rack position: where the barbell sits across the weightlifter's chest at the end of the clean movement in the clean and jerk.

Squat: a lift where competitors take the barbell across their shoulders and bend their legs to look like they are sitting.

For safety reasons, powerlifters may have someone to help, or "spot," them during a lift.

Gymnastics

The sport of gymnastics has changed a lot since the ancient Greeks performed routines naked. Today's gymnasts compete on a variety of apparatus, with each one requiring different skills and abilities from the gymnast.

Pommel horse

Only men compete on the pommel horse. The pommel horse itself is 5 ft 2 in (1.6 m) long and 3 ft 5 in (1.05 m) from the top of the safety mat. During a routine, gymnasts must perform a smooth, continuous chain of movements using all parts of the horse.

Only women compete on the beam.

Aim of the game

Gymnasts compete on a range of apparatus to score the highest points. The gymnast who finishes with the highest points on each apparatus comes first.

Men and women are judged in the same way whatever apparatus they are using.

There are two different panels judging each routine. The first awards points for the compulsory elements (the moves that must be included). The second score is a mark out of 10 for the routine. The two scores are then added together.

To compete at the Olympic games, gymnasts must be at least 16 years old.

The beam

Each gymnast has up to 90 seconds to impress the judges with a performance on the balance beam. The beam is 4 ft 1 in (1.25 m) high and 16 ft 5 in (5 m) long, but just 4 in (10 cm) wide. Gymnasts score more points for a wide range of acrobatic jumps, leaps, and turns along the entire length of the beam. The routine must also include different sitting, standing, and lying positions, and show elegance, rhythm, and balance.

The two handles, or pommels are 16–18 in (40–45 cm) apart.

All moves, such as the scissors, must be perfect to score a high mark.

Vault

In the vault, gymnasts have a run-up of 82 ft (25 m) before leaping off a springboard onto the vault table. The springboard gives them the height to complete moves in midair, including tucks and pikes, before landing on both feet.

From takeoff to landing, a vault performance takes about two seconds.

The bars

There are different sets of bars in gymnastics. Women compete on uneven bars (two bars of different heights) and men on the high bar and parallel bars. Uneven and high bar routines include somersaults and twists, and end with a spectacular dismount. The parallel bars combines swinging movements with shows of strength, where the gymnast holds himself still.

Gymnasts must use the entire length of the parallel bars to score high points.

The rings

To compete on the rings successfully, gymnasts need to be strong and have an amazing sense of balance. A routine on the rings should include a series of swings and holds, and finish with an acrobatic dismount. The rings hang 9 ft (2.8 m) above the floor.

A rings routine includes static moves, where the gymnast holds himself still, such as this iron cross.

On the floor

Rhythmic and acrobatic gymnasts aim to impress the judges with their grace and rhythm. Routines include dazzling moves as gymnasts combine dance steps with acrobatic tumbles and turns.

Jargon buster

Punch: when a gymnast bounces off the floor or a piece of apparatus rather than jumps.

Salto: another word for a somersault or flip.

Stick: when a gymnast lands without having to take an extra step for balance.

V-sit: a position where the legs are held together and raised above the head, forming a "V" shape, while the body is held off the floor by the hands.

Floor routine

Floor routines are performed by individual male and female gymnasts. Women's routines last for 90 seconds and they combine dance moves with tumbling and acrobatics. Male gymnasts' routines last for 60 seconds. They must show strength and balance, combining moves such as somersaults and twists. Floor gymnasts are penalized if they do not use the whole floor area during their routine.

Rhythmic gymnastics

Rhythmic gymnasts take part as individuals or as a team of five. Gymnasts perform to music and mix gymnastic moves with dance. Gymnasts also perform with a piece of hand apparatus—a ball, clubs, hoop, ribbon, or rope. Each routine is marked on its difficulty, presentation, and how well the apparatus is used.

Gymnasts can pass through the hoop or spin and rotate it on a part of the body.

Aim of the game

Floor gymnasts combine elements of dance and gymnastics in their floor routines.

A routine takes place on a sprung square floor that is 39 ft x 39 ft (12 m x 12 m). Competitors are not allowed to step out of the floor area.

The gymnast's routine is scored by a panel of judges.

A solo rhythmic gymnastics routine is up to 1 minute 30 seconds long, while a team routine is up to 2 minutes 30 seconds long.

In rhythmic routines, gymnasts are not allowed to keep hold of the ball apparatus.

Those performing with the ribbon must keep the ribbon moving at all times.

Acrobatics competitions involve teams of up to four competitors. Teams have 2 minutes 30 seconds to perform their routines.

Acrobatic gymnastics

Acrobatic gymnasts combine dance with complicated acrobatic moves such as somersaults, balances, and holds. The sport is performed on a standard gymnastics floor by male, female, or mixed pairs, or groups of four.

Female gymnasts perform their floor routine to music.

The boundary line marks the edge of the floor area.

Gymnasts should keep their toes pointed when performing leaps, springs, and poses

The gymnast twirls the ribbon to form patterns in the air, including snakes, spirals, and arcs.

Handling apparatus

Each piece of hand apparatus used by rhythmic gymnasts has a set of rules that control its use. The ball must be balanced, rolled, or thrown into the air, but never held. The rope can be held or wrapped around the body, and the clubs must be thrown as the gymnast tumbles and moves across the floor.

Target sports

Whether striking a ball toward a hole or shooting an arrow at a board, athletes competing in target sports perform under extreme pressure. They need to have nerves of steel and superb eye-hand coordination so that they can hit the target time after time.

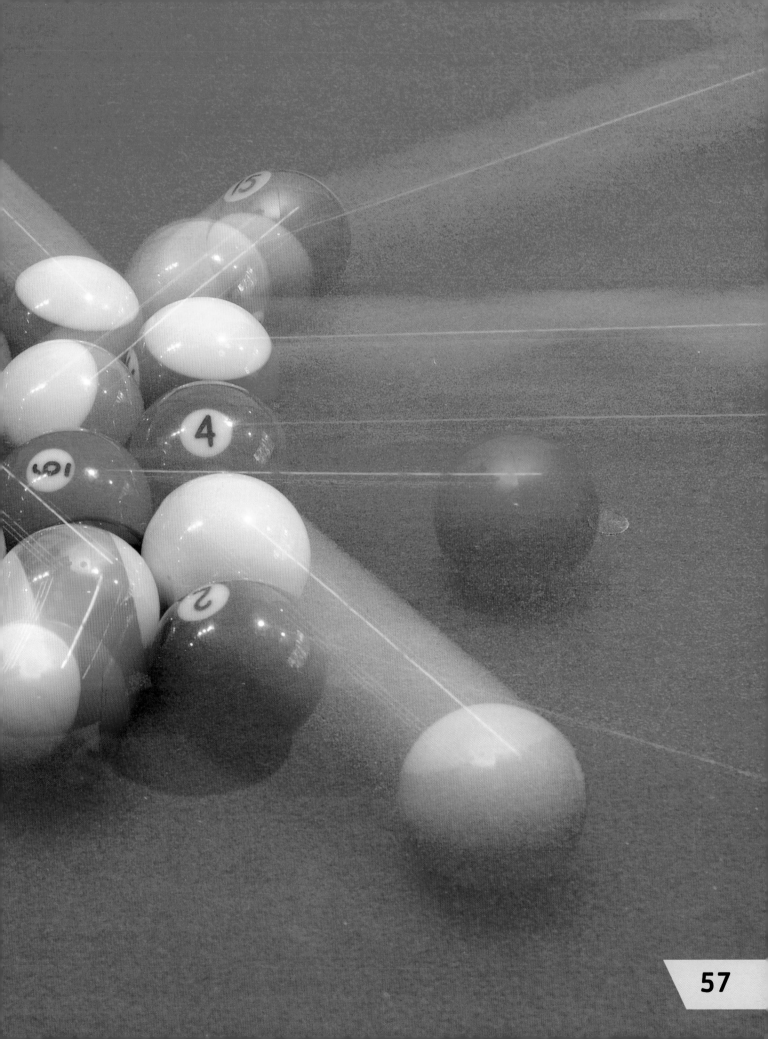

Golf

Golf involves hitting a small ball a long way into a small hole using as few shots (called strokes) as possible. It might look straightforward, but it requires great skill and concentration, as well as many hours of practice.

This golfer is hitting her tee shot over a water hazard and toward the green in the distance.

From the tee to the green

A round of golf is made up of nine or 18 holes. The first shot of a golf hole is played from an area called the tee box. Most golfers use a small support, called a tee, to lift the ball off the grass. This gives the golfer more control over the ball. Using a club, golfers aim to hit the ball along a path of short grass called the fairway. This runs from the tee box up to the green, which is the area of very short grass that sits around the hole itself.

Avoiding hazards

Every golf hole is different. Some are longer than others; some are straight and some have bends; and they have different obstacles, called hazards. These are designed to trap golfers so that they have to play extra shots to get out of them. Hazards include streams and sand-filled pits, called sand traps or bunkers.

Jargon buster

Hole: the name given to each section of a golf course from the tee area to the green. It is also the target that golfers aim at.

Par: how many strokes it should take to play a particular hole.

Putt: a short, light stroke that makes the ball roll along the ground.

Stroke: another word for a shot.

Tee: a small peg made of wood or plastic 2–4 in (5–10 cm) high. The ball is played off a tee on the first stroke of a hole (also called the tee shot).

Judging a putt

Once the golfer has the ball on the green, he or she must putt the ball to sink it into the hole. Golfers must be able to "read" the green. They look closely at the surface to spot any slopes and dips. They will then try to judge how the ball will roll toward the hole after it has been hit.

A golf hole is only 4¼ in (10.8 cm) wide, so golfers need to putt accurately to hit the target.

The flag sits in the hole and gives golfers a target to aim at.

A golfer must hit a ball into a hole using the fewest number of strokes. A round of golf may have nine or 18 holes.

Each golf hole starts with the golfer hitting the ball off a tee and ends when he or she putts the ball into the hole.

Each golf hole is given a rating of how many shots it would take a very good golfer to play it. This is called par.

If the golfer takes one shot over (more than) par, it is called a bogie. A score of two shots over par is called a double bogie.

One shot under par is called a birdie. Two shots under par is called an eagle. Scoring three shots under par is called a double eagle.

If the ball lands in a hazard, golfers can play the ball or take a shot penalty, which means they can move the ball but must add a stroke to their score.

Some holes have markers showing the edge of the playing area. If the ball travels beyond these it is "out of bounds." The golfer must replay the shot and he or she is penalized a stroke.

The essentials

Golfers usually carry three types of golf club. Putters are used for putting. Woods are used for long-distance shots, such as the first shot off the tee area. Irons are used for shots between the tee area and the green and to get out of hazards.

Areas of rough sit on each side of the fairway.

Green

Dimples on the golf ball help it to fly through the air.

Tee box

Bunker

Fairway

Hole

Woods have a thick head.

The length of each hole is measured in yards from the tee to the green.

Golfers carry only one putter.

Irons have a thin metal head, called the blade.

59

Aim of the game

A curling match is played between two teams of four players. The players are called the lead, the second, the third, and the skip.

Each player plays two stones. Once all 16 stones have been played, it is called an "end."

The team whose stone is closest to the center of the house scores one point. The team scores an extra point for each stone they have nearer the center than their opponents' stones.

The team with the most points wins the match.

A match lasts two hours and 15 minutes or until a total of 10 ends are completed.

The team that wins the end plays first in the next end.

Sweepers are not allowed to touch the stone with their brushes. If this happens, the stone is taken out of play.

Curling

First played in Scotland in 1541, curling is now played on ice rinks around the world. Competitors must have a good aim and use clever tactics to defeat opponents.

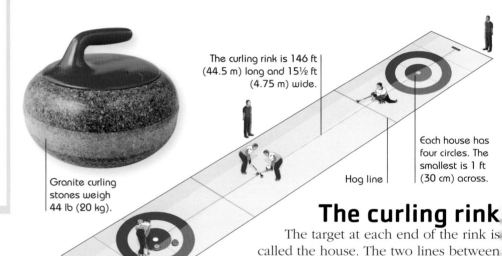

Granite curling stones weigh 44 lb (20 kg).

The curling rink is 146 ft (44.5 m) long and 15½ ft (4.75 m) wide.

Each house has four circles. The smallest is 1 ft (30 cm) across.

Hog line

Taking aim

Teams aim to slide their eight curling stones onto the house to score points. Teams can also use their stones to protect their point-scoring stones. This type of shot is called a guard shot. They can also knock an opponent's stone off the house using a strike shot.

The curling rink

The target at each end of the rink is called the house. The two lines between each house are called the hog lines. Players must release the stones before they reach the first hog line. Once the curling stone is released, teammates use brushes to sweep in front of the stone to melt the ice. This alters the path of the curling stone so teams can guide it onto the house.

Curlers keep their eyes on the house as they deliver their stone.

Special shoes with one smooth and one gripping sole help players to slide when delivering a stone.

Balance

Bowls

The world's oldest bowling green is in Southampton, UK, and has been used since 1299. Today, bowls can be played both indoors and outdoors.

Bowls are round with flattened sides.

The jack is a sphere that is 2½ in (6.35 cm) wide.

The jack is rolled to the far end of the rink.

The red bowl to the right of the jack is nearest and its bowler will score one point.

The rink

A bowling green is divided into playing strips called rinks. The player who wins a coin toss rolls a small ball, called the jack, down the rink. The jack is the target that bowlers try to get their bowls as close to as possible.

Targeting the jack

Bowls are not completely round, so they do not move in straight lines. To roll them accurately, players must judge how much they will curve. They use several types of delivery to get the bowls as close to the jack as possible. The draw shot starts out wide and curves into the jack. In a strike delivery, players aim to knock the jack or an opponent's bowl out of play. A block is a bowl placed short to stop an opponent's draw shot.

Aim of the game

A game of bowls is played by two opposing single players or teams. Teams are made up of two bowlers (pairs), three bowlers (triples), or four bowlers (fours).

In a singles game, each player has four bowls to roll at the jack. Once all eight bowls have been rolled, it is called an "end."

A match is made up of 18 ends or until a team or player reaches a preset points total.

The player or team whose bowl is closest to the jack scores one point. They score an extra point for each bowl they have nearer to the jack than their opponents' bowls.

Aim of the game

Bowlers try to knock down 10 wooden pins by rolling a ball down a lane toward the pins.

Each pin knocked down is worth one point.

The player who scores the most points during a game wins.

Players take turns bowling frames. Each frame is made up of two rolls of the ball.

There are 10 frames in a game.

If the ball is not thrown accurately, it can roll into the gutter before reaching the pins, leaving the bowler with a score of zero for that throw.

Ten-pin

One of the world's most popular pastimes, ten-pin bowling has been played for thousands of years. In the early 20th century, toy bowling balls and pins were discovered in the grave of an Egyptian child dating from about 5200 BCE.

Get a grip!

There are three finger holes at the top of each ball. Two of the holes are for the player's ring and middle finger. The third hole is for the player's thumb. While beginners will use all three holes, many professional players use just two fingers to hold the ball, leaving their thumb out of the hole. This gives them greater control over the ball.

The bowler pulls the ball back before releasing it. This is called the backlift.

The essentials

A bowling lane is made up of the approach area at one end and the pin deck at the other. Bowlers stand behind the foul line on the approach area to roll the ball down the lane at the pins. Balls can vary in size and weight, but they must be no more than 2 ft 3 in (69 cm) in circumference and can weigh up to 16 lb (7.26 kg).

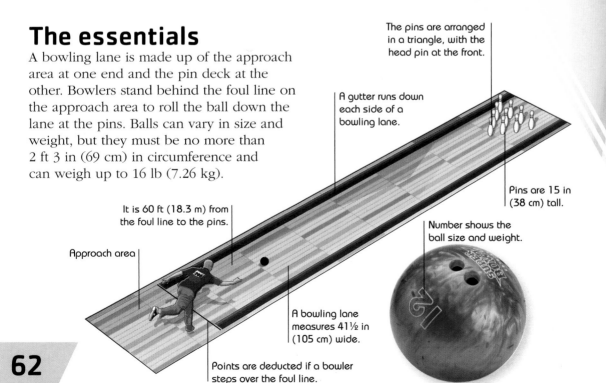

The pins are arranged in a triangle, with the head pin at the front.

A gutter runs down each side of a bowling lane.

Pins are 15 in (38 cm) tall.

Number shows the ball size and weight.

It is 60 ft (18.3 m) from the foul line to the pins.

Approach area

A bowling lane measures 41½ in (105 cm) wide.

Points are deducted if a bowler steps over the foul line.

Strike time

Bowlers earn extra points with strikes and spares. A strike is when all the pins are knocked down in the first roll of frame. Bonus points are added depending on what is scored in the next two rolls (if they knock down five and two pins, they get seven extra points). A spare is when all 10 pins are knocked down in two rolls. Bonus points depend on what is scored with the next roll.

If a player scores a strike in each frame, he or she will reach the maximum score of 300.

Bowling technique

Good technique is key to ten-pin success. Some bowlers aim the ball straight into the head pin (the pin at the front). Other players roll hook balls, where the ball curves in toward the pins as it travels. A hook ball for a right-handed player curves from right to left. They do this by flicking their fingers as they deliver the ball so that it spins as it rolls down the lane.

Jargon buster

Backup ball: a ball that curves in the opposite direction of a hook ball. A backup ball for a right-handed bowler will curve from left to right.

Cranker: a bowler who makes the ball spin more than usual and so it swerves across a lane.

Split: when two or more pins are left standing and they are not next to each other.

Turkey: a word used to describe three strikes in a row. It is also called a triple.

Wood: a pin that is standing directly behind another one, making it difficult to see.

Bowlers wear special shoes so they do not damage the lane.

Snooker

A sport of skill and intense concentration, snooker has grown in popularity since it was first played in the 19th century by British soldiers based in India.

Aim of the game

Snooker is played on a special table with pockets in each of the corners and two more halfway down the sides.

Players score points by hitting the white ball (cue ball) so that it knocks one of the colored balls into a pocket. This is called potting.

If they successfully pot a ball, they can play another shot. The number of points scored in one visit to the table is called a break. When a player fails to make a pot, his or her opponent takes over.

Players must pot a red ball first. They can then pot one of the colored balls. If successful, the colored ball is put back on the table and the player tries to pot another red ball. When all the red balls have been potted, the colored balls are potted in order of their points.

On the baize

Matches are divided into frames. A frame lasts from the first shot until a player wins. Players can try to "snooker" their opponents by blocking a colored ball with another ball. These difficult shots often result in players making a foul shot and giving points to their opponents. Fouls occur if a player misses the ball, pots a ball that he is not supposed to pot, pots the cue ball, or touches the cue ball more than once. It is also a foul if any ball jumps off the table.

Cue ball

Red: 1 point

Yellow: 2 points

Green: 3 points

Brown: 4 points

Blue: 5 points

Pink: 6 points

Black: 7 points

At the start of a frame, the balls are always placed as shown here.

Cue ball

Pink ball

There are 15 red balls to be potted.

Pocket

Balls and table

A snooker table is 12 ft (3.56 m) long and 6 ft (1.78 m) wide. It is covered with a special fabric called baize. There are 21 colored balls and a white cue ball. Each colored ball is worth a different number of points, with black having the highest value and red the lowest.

Balls measure 2 in (5.2 cm) in diameter and are made from hard plastic.

Players use one hand as a bridge to support the cue while playing a shot.

Pool

Played on a smaller table than snooker, eight-ball pool matches are fast-paced games where players try to pocket their balls before their opponents.

The cue ball is slightly smaller than the other balls.

At the start of each frame, the balls are arranged, or "racked," using a wooden triangle.

Ball basics

Pool is played with a cue ball and 15 object balls. Players try to pocket eight balls. Seven of the object balls are a solid color and seven are striped. The eight ball is solid black. The table is 7 ft 8 in (2.3 m) or 8 ft 4 in (2.5 m) long and 3 ft 10 in (1.1 m) or 4 ft 2 in (1.3 m) wide. There are six pockets—four in the corners and two halfway along the sides.

Players chalk the tips of their cues to give them greater control over the cue ball.

Aim of the game

Pool is usually played by two players, but it can be played by more players who work together in teams.

Players hit the cue ball so that it knocks the other balls into the pockets. They can only hit the cue ball with their cues.

Once the first ball has been pocketed, players then stick to pocketing either the solid balls or the striped balls. If a player pockets a solid ball first, then he or she must sink all the solid balls on the table.

When all seven of the player's balls have been pocketed, he or she must pocket the black eight ball into a chosen pocket to win.

If a player pockets the eight ball before pocketing all of his or her own balls, he or she will automatically lose the game.

If a shot fails to hit any ball or the player pockets the cue ball, the opponent is awarded a free shot or can place the cue ball anywhere on the table.

Pool variations

In addition to eight-ball pool, nine-ball pool and straight pool are also played. A nine-ball game is played with a cue ball and nine numbered balls. Players must pocket the balls in number order, with the one ball pocketed first and the nine ball last. In straight pool, players get a point for each ball pocketed.

Archery

Patience, nerve, a sharp eye, and a steady hand are needed to be successful at archery. Today, the sport is played in more than 140 countries around the world, and archery competitions are closely fought events that can go down to the very last arrow.

Eyes on the prize

Archery competitions are held over a variety of distances, both indoors and outdoors. There are also different types of archery. Target archery sees archers fire a number of arrows at targets. The targets are then moved to a different distance, and the archers shoot another set of arrows. In field archery, the archers move around a course, shooting at static (non-moving) targets, which are sometimes shaped like animals.

Aim of the game

 Archers use a bow to shoot arrows at a target.

The target is made up of a series of circles and each circle is worth different points.

The archer with the highest score wins the match.

In competition, archers shoot three or six arrows during each turn. A turn is called an end and the ends make up a round. The number of ends in a competition varies. In an indoor match, 20 ends are shot.

Archers wait for the command to begin and have a time limit to shoot their arrows.

Once all the arrows are shot, archers then add up their scores.

Stabilizers help to keep the bow steady during a shot.

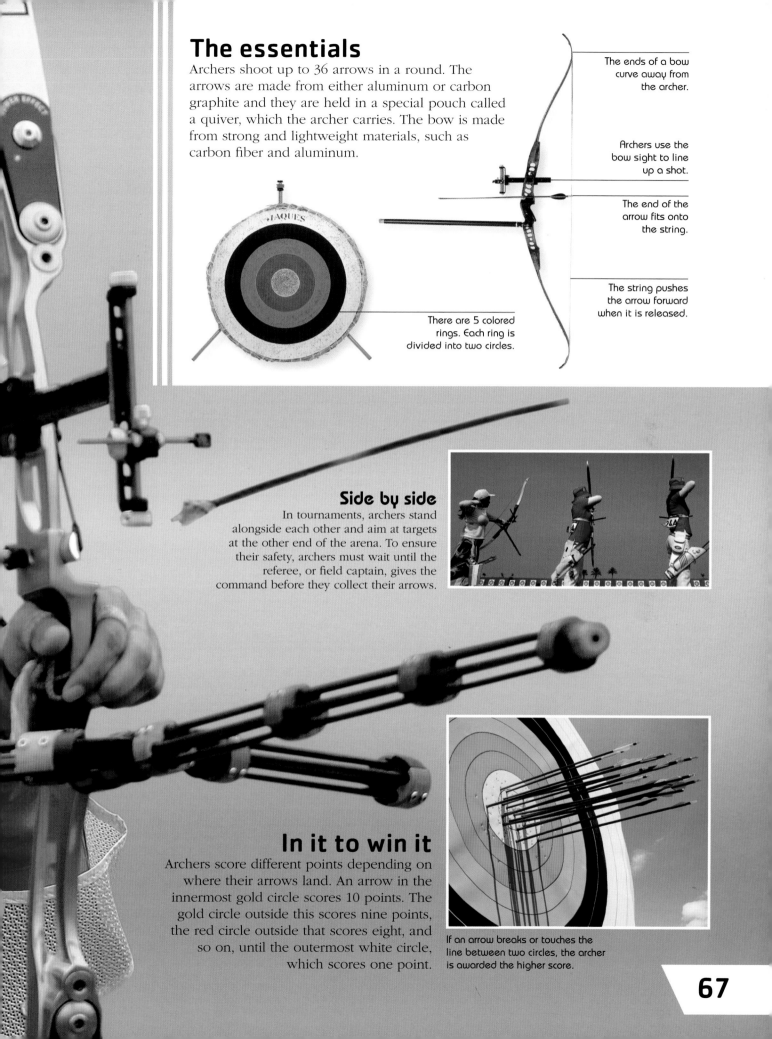

The essentials

Archers shoot up to 36 arrows in a round. The arrows are made from either aluminum or carbon graphite and they are held in a special pouch called a quiver, which the archer carries. The bow is made from strong and lightweight materials, such as carbon fiber and aluminum.

The ends of a bow curve away from the archer.

Archers use the bow sight to line up a shot.

The end of the arrow fits onto the string.

The string pushes the arrow forward when it is released.

There are 5 colored rings. Each ring is divided into two circles.

Side by side

In tournaments, archers stand alongside each other and aim at targets at the other end of the arena. To ensure their safety, archers must wait until the referee, or field captain, gives the command before they collect their arrows.

In it to win it

Archers score different points depending on where their arrows land. An arrow in the innermost gold circle scores 10 points. The gold circle outside this scores nine points, the red circle outside that scores eight, and so on, until the outermost white circle, which scores one point.

If an arrow breaks or touches the line between two circles, the archer is awarded the higher score.

Aiming high

The challenge of good target sports is to hit those hard-to-reach places. You might expect arrows, darts, and balls to be used in these sports, but have you tried horseshoes and lasers?

A dart is 6–8 in (15–20 cm) long. The rear end has a stabilizing set of four wings, known as the flight.

Rifle shooting

Competitors need a steady hand to hit tiny targets 11 yd to 1,000 yd (10 m to 915 m) away. Some rifle competitions also mark the shooter on speed.

Croquet

This game of accuracy is played on a grass lawn. Players use a mallet to strike their pair of balls through a circuit of six hoops. To win, the player must then hit a central peg with both balls.

Petanque

Petanque players aim to throw hollow metal balls at a target ball known as a jack. The player must stand with both feet in a starting circle to register a legal throw. Petanque is usually played on a hard dirt field.

Darts

Competitors throw three darts at a circular board that is split into 62 sections, each worth a different amount of points. Players subtract their scored points from 501 points until they reach zero.

English billiards

This is played on a table with six pockets. Only three balls are used, two of which are cue balls (one for each player). Points are scored by hitting the other balls in one shot or knocking them into a pocket.

Horseshoes

Players throw a horseshoe at a target stake 13 yd (12 m) away. A player scores three points when the horseshoe lands around the stake, or one point for getting it close (a "near miss").

Pistol shooting

Shooters use a handgun to fire at a small target to score points. Pistol shooting is also the first event of the modern pentathlon, and uses special laser pistols.

Water sports

A variety of sports take place in or on water. Swimmers glide through the pool as quickly as possible, while divers move with elegance and grace to enter the water. In contrast, rowing, kayaking, and sailing are tests of strength and stamina as athletes battle against currents and tides to be the best in their sport.

Swimming

Swimming races are held in a pool or in open-water courses in lakes and rivers. They can be short bursts of speed over a single length, or tiring endurance races.

Swimmers must swim through the water without touching the bottom of the pool.

In competitions, swimmers race against each other over a set distance using a specific stroke.

The four competition strokes are freestyle (front crawl), butterfly, breaststroke, and backstroke.

Swimmers are not allowed to swim out of their lanes. If they do, they will be disqualified.

At the end of each length, swimmers must touch a special pad before they turn, otherwise they will be disqualified.

In an individual medley, swimmers compete over 200 m (656 ft) or 400 m (1,312 ft). They must swim all four strokes in this order: butterfly, backstroke, breaststroke, and freestyle.

In a team medley relay, different swimmers perform the strokes in this order: backstroke, breaststroke, butterfly, and freestyle.

Relays for individual strokes can also take place over 200 m (636 ft) and 400 m (1,272 ft).

Swimmers launch themselves into the pool off starting blocks.

A good start

Swimmers competing in the breaststroke, freestyle, and butterfly races dive into the water from starting blocks, making their bodies as streamlined as possible. Then they glide under the water for a short distance before rising to the surface to begin their stroke. Backstroke swimmers start their races in the pool, launching themselves backward from the pool's edge.

Jargon buster

Freestyle: a type of race where swimmers can use any stroke they want. Most swimmers use front crawl because this is the fastest stroke.

Long course: a swimming pool 50 m (164 ft) long.

Medley: a race that includes all four swimming strokes.

Open water: ponds, rivers, and lakes.

Short course: a swimming pool 25 m (82 ft) long .

In the swim

Open-water races usually take place over 10 km (6.2 miles) or 25 km (15.5 miles). Open-water swimming also forms part of some multiple sport events, such as the triathlon. In pool-based events, swimmers race over distances from 50 m (164 ft) up to 1,500 m (4,921 ft). These races may feature just one stroke, or swimmers may be required to perform all four strokes, one after the other, in races called medleys.

The essentials

In addition to timing judges, pools have touch pads to record the swimmer's time. To help them go faster and reduce their finishing times, most swimmers wear caps, and even shave their bodies!

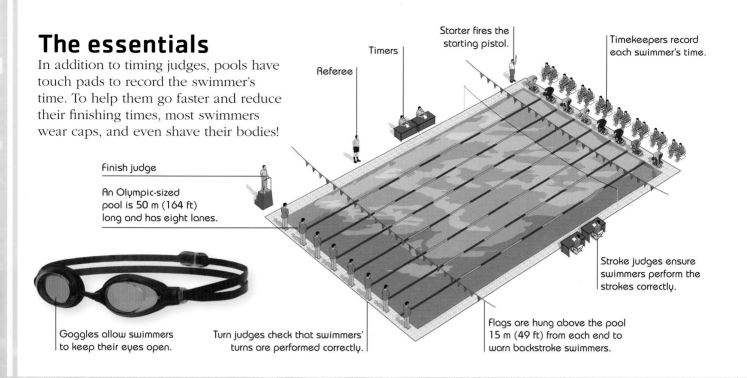

Referee

Timers

Starter fires the starting pistol.

Timekeepers record each swimmer's time.

Finish judge

An Olympic-sized pool is 50 m (164 ft) long and has eight lanes.

Goggles allow swimmers to keep their eyes open.

Turn judges check that swimmers' turns are performed correctly.

Stroke judges ensure swimmers perform the strokes correctly.

Flags are hung above the pool 15 m (49 ft) from each end to warn backstroke swimmers.

Butterfly is one of the hardest strokes to perform—it takes a great deal of coordination between a swimmer's arms, legs, and body.

Different strokes

Butterfly, breaststroke, and front crawl are all performed on a swimmer's front, but backstroke is swum face-up. In front crawl and backstroke, swimmers swing their arms out of the water one at a time. In butterfly, both arms lift out of the water at the same time. In breaststroke, the arms stay in the water at all times, pushing forward and then pulling back to the swimmer's sides.

Backstroke swimmers bring their arms over their heads alternately with each stroke.

73

Diving

It takes bravery and skill to make a dive from the edge of a platform 10 m (32 ft) above a pool. Divers need to be fast, flexible, and strong to perform acrobatic moves and hold the correct body positions before entering the water as cleanly as possible.

Divers can launch themselves from the board facing backward, forward, or even from a handstand.

Diving for points

Divers choose from a number of dives that have different degrees (levels) of difficulty. Competition dives are marked out of 10. Judges award up to three points each for the takeoff, flight, and entry into the water, and another point on how well the dive was performed. The highest and lowest judges' scores are ignored. The remaining scores are added together and multiplied by the degree of difficulty to give the final score.

Aim of the game

Divers jump from platforms or springboards into a swimming or diving pool.

Jumps include acrobatic moves, such as somersaults, tucks, and twists.

Diving is done singly or in pairs.

Before a competition, divers are told which features their dives must include. They then send officials a list of their dives. At the competition, divers must complete only the dives on their approved list. If they do not, they will score zero.

There are between five and seven judges who award scores depending on the difficulty and skill of the dive.

The diver with the highest score wins the competition.

Degree of difficulty: a measure of how hard a dive is to complete. Degree of difficulty is sometimes shown as "DD" on a diving scorecard.

Flight: the part of the dive after the diver has taken off from the platform or springboard and before he or she enters the pool.

Handsprings: when divers use their hands to launch from the board or platform.

Springboard: a type of diving board that acts like a spring and bends as divers jump on it.

The essentials

Divers jump from platforms and springboards at different heights. At the Olympics, divers use the 10-meter platform and the 3-meter springboard. The stairs to the springboards and platforms are nonslip for safety.

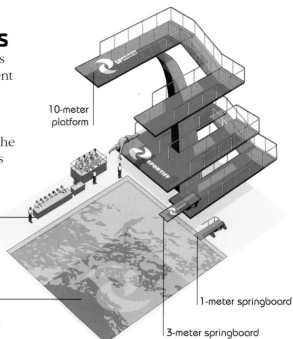

10-meter platform

Panel of judges sits on the poolside.

Water jets are sprayed across the water's surface.

1-meter springboard

3-meter springboard

Tuck and turn

Divers can use a number of positions when they dive from the board. In a tuck position, divers curl their body into a tight ball. In a straight position, the body is not bent at all. These positions are combined with different moves, including somersaults and twists.

In the pike position, divers bend their body at the hips, keeping their legs straight and their feet together.

Synchronized divers are judged on how precisely they move at the same time.

Divers enter hands-first to reduce the amount of splash they make.

Splashdown

Diving into a pool can be dangerous, so water is sprayed across the pool's surface to minimize the force of the diver's impact. All divers aim to enter the water with as small a splash as possible. This is called a rip. The smaller the splash, the higher the points awarded.

Diving as one

In synchronized diving, two divers perform at the same time. They perform either exactly the same moves, or mirror-image moves. As in individual events, judges mark the dive, and the pair's score is then multiplied by the degree of difficulty to give a final score.

Rowing

A sport of power and pace, rowers need to be fit and strong to compete at the highest level. Competition can be fierce and races usually end in a lung-bursting surge for the finish.

Aim of the game

Rowers travel backward in a boat using oars to move as fast as possible.

Races are held over various distances on lakes and rivers.

Olympic rowing races take place over a straight course that is 2 km (1.4 miles) long. The course is divided up into lanes, and each boat must stay in its own lane.

At the start of a race, boats line up at the ends of small piers, called pontoons.

The first boat to cross the finish line wins the race.

The cox sits at the back of the boat, facing forward. He or she steers the boat and calls out the rowing pace and race tactics.

Sweeping and sculling

There are two types of rowing race. Rowing with one oar per rower is called sweeping, while rowing with two oars per rower is called sculling. Both sweeping and sculling boats can have two, four, or eight rowers in them. There are also sculling races for individual rowers.

A sculling oar is usually 10 ft (3 m) long.

Acting as one

It is vital that all the rowers on a boat row together to power the boat through the water as quickly as possible. If the boat does not have a cox, the other rowers take their pace from the rower at the back, who is called the stroke. Sweeping and sculling oars are long and lightweight with a large blade at one end.

Kayaking

From racing through choppy water in the slalom to fast-paced sprints, kayaking requires extreme fitness and stamina, as well as great technical skill.

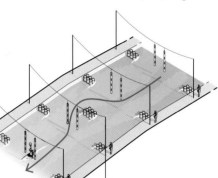

A slalom kayak is 13 ft (4 m) long.

Artificial hazards line the slalom course.

Judges check that gates are passed correctly.

A slalom gate is made up of two poles hanging from a wire.

Through the gate

Like rowing, some kayaking races take place on flat courses over 500 m (547 yd) and 10,000 m (10,936 yd). Slalom events are held on artificial courses with fast-flowing water, hazards, and gates. Kayakers must travel through the gates in the correct order and direction, without touching them.

Aim of the game

Kayakers use paddles to move their boats forward over a body of water.

Races can take place on a flat course over different distances or on white water. This is fast-flowing water that is frothy and has lots of waves.

There are also races for teams of two or four kayakers.

The first kayak in a flat course race to cross the finish line wins.

In white-water slalom kayaking, kayakers race against the clock on their own. They have two chances to go down the course. The kayaker with the fastest time wins the race.

Making a splash

Kayakers use their whole body to control their kayak. They will paddle with their arms and twist their legs and bodies to steer the kayak over straight lines and around tight bends. Kayakers also need to be able to roll their kayak right over should it flip over (capsize).

Paddles have curved blades at either end to catch the water.

Sailing

Using just the wind to push them through the water, sailors brave the elements to steer their yachts skillfully around a course. The sport is physically and mentally demanding, and sailors must be able to act quickly to avoid disaster.

All at sea

Ocean racing is the ultimate challenge for sailors. These races cross the biggest oceans and some even sail around the world. Racing can also take place close to the coastline, in offshore racing. However, not all sailing races take place on the sea. In some competitions, such as the Olympics, temporary courses are marked out on lakes using inflatable markers called buoys.

Aim of the game

Sailors must sail a yacht around a course using only the wind.

The first yacht to reach the finish line is the winner.

Sailors must avoid collisions with other yachts at all costs.

If a yacht causes an infringement (breaks a rule), another yacht can raise a red flag to protest. The judges take evidence from both yachts after the race to make a ruling.

If another yacht is in danger, sailors have a duty to help that yacht, even if it costs them the race.

A sailor controls the rudder on a small yacht using a rod called the tiller.

Catch the wind

At the start of a race, sailors usually sail into the wind. To do this, they use a zigzag course, which is known as beating. Race starts can see yachts in close competition as sailors battle to get the best position and make the most of the wind.

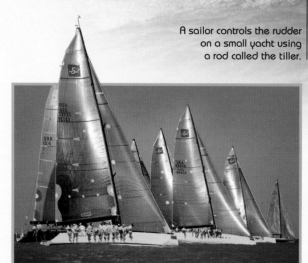

Yachts clump together at the start of an offshore race.

Sails catch the wind to push a yacht forward.

Jargon buster

Boom: a horizontal pole that is fixed to the bottom of a sail.

Hull: the body of a boat. Yachts can have one hull (monohull), two hulls (catamaran), or even three hulls (trimaran).

Keel: a thin blade that sticks into the water to stop the boat from drifting sideways.

Mast: a tall vertical pole onto which the sails are fixed.

Rudder: a thin blade at the back of the boat. It is moved from side to side to steer the boat.

The three hulls of this ocean-racing trimaran are linked by strong arms and netting, which the sailors use to cross from hull to hull.

Types of boat

Sailing boats come in many different shapes and sizes. One of the most popular types is the laser yacht. These are used for single-handed sailing. Large ocean racers are designed for rough seas and used in around-the-world races. Competition boats have large sails and are usually made of lightweight materials, such as fiberglass, aluminum, and carbon fiber.

The essentials

Sailors wear different clothing to suit the race type and weather conditions. For competitions near the shore and on lakes, they wear a wet suit and a buoyancy aid. For offshore competitions and ocean racing, they need clothing that is more protective, such as thick jackets, yachting boots, overalls, and a life jacket.

Buoyancy aids help to keep sailors afloat if they fall in the water.

Wet suits can cover the whole body or leave arms and legs bare.

Life jackets keep sailors face-up if they fall in the water.

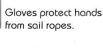

Gloves protect hands from sail ropes.

Boots help to grip the deck.

Windsurfing

Professionals can reach speeds of up to 50 mph (80 kph) on their windsurfers. But windsurfing is about more than speed: freestyle competitors perform tricks as skillfully and stylishly as possible.

Doing tricks

Wave windsurfing and freestyle windsurfing involve acrobatic tricks. In wave windsurfing, competitors must ride waves and jump them as they break. They can then perform tricks, such as loops. Freestyle windsurfing developed from wave windsurfing. In freestyle events, competitors have a time limit to perform as many tricks as possible. They are judged on their skill and the number of tricks performed.

Competitors need strength in their legs and upper body to stay on the board.

A freestyle board can weigh as little as 11 lb (5 kg).

Aim of the game

In all windsurfing contests, competitors must stay on the board as they windsurf.

Wave and freestyle competitors must perform tricks without falling off the board. Judges mark them on their skill and creativity. The competitor with the highest points wins.

Wave and freestyle competitors coming back to the shore must give way to those going out.

In Olympic and formula racing, the competitor who completes the course in the fastest time wins the race.

Speed sailing competitors complete a course twice against the clock. The times for each race are averaged out. The competitor with the lowest average time wins the race.

Right tools for the job

Competitors use different types of board and sail for different competitions. In the Olympic Games, all competitors must use windsurfers made to the same specifications. Wave and freestyle competitors use shorter boards and smaller sails, which make it easier to perform tricks.

Racing windsurfers usually have large sails to catch the most wind so they move faster.

Clear panels allow the competitor to see what is happening.

Racing

In windsurfing races, including speed sailing and Olympic events, competitors race around a set course. The course will make the best of the wind and is marked out by large floats, called buoys.

Competitors race together as a fleet at the start of an international event.

The essentials

Windsurfers have a board and sail. The length of both varies, depending on the competition. Competitors also wear different outfits for different conditions, from full-length wet suits for cold water, to shorts and a shirt for warm conditions.

Foot straps ensure board and competitor are not separated.

Shoes provide extra grip on the board.

Stiff battens keep the sail tight.

Wet suits keep the competitors warm in cold water.

Aim of the game

Surfers use a surfboard to ride waves for as long as possible.

In a competition, two or four surfers compete at the same time. They are usually given 20 minutes to ride the waves and impress the judges.

In an event where four surfers compete at the same time, only the top two surfers will go through to the next round of the event.

Points are awarded for the choice of wave (the harder the wave is to ride, the more points scored), and the position on the wave (riding on the crest of the wave is better).

The time on the wave and the quality of any tricks performed is also important.

The surfer with the highest points wins the competition.

There are separate events for male and female surfers.

Surfing

Surfing was invented hundreds of years ago by the islanders of the Pacific Ocean. The sport has hardly changed since then—a surfer still uses a board to brave the waves. The bigger the waves, the bigger the thrills.

Best foot forward

The natural way to ride a surfboard is with the left foot forward. Riding the board with the right foot forward is known as "goofy footed." In addition to the stance, there are two ways to tackle a wave. Facing into the wave is called forehand and facing away from the wave is called backhand. While the board position is important, it is what surfers do when they are on the board that counts in a competition.

Riding the waves

In a competition, several surfers take to the water at the same time. Once a surfer is standing on the board, the judges will count that as a wave, and start to mark the surfer. A score out of 10 is given to the surfer. At the end of the session, the judges add up the surfer's three best waves to get a total score.

Surfers try to stay on the wave for as long as possible. Once the wave crashes over, which is called breaking, they will skim over the foam, known as soup.

This longboarder is wearing a helmet for extra protection on the waves.

Shirts protect surfers from the harsh sun.

Long and short of it

Surfers can choose to ride either a longboard or a shortboard. Longboards can be up to 12 ft (3.7 m) long, while shortboards can be just 5 ft (1.5 m). Longboards are more stable in the water than shortboards, but they are more difficult to turn. Professional surfers usually prefer shortboards, because they are lighter, turn quicker, and it is easier to do tricks on them. However, there are longboard categories for professionals in some international competitions.

The essentials

Surfboards are made from lightweight materials, such as polystyrene and fiberglass. There are fins on the underside of the board to keep it stable in the water. A safety leash links the surfer to the board so they do not become separated. Surfers wear wet suits to keep them warm in colder weather.

The top of the surfboard is called the deck.

The front of the board is called the nose.

The back of the board is called the tail.

A thin strip of wood called the stringer runs down the middle and increases the strength of the board.

The leash is fitted around the ankle or wrist.

More splash

Water sports are a blend of elegance, power, and speed. If you love the water and want to try something a little different, then check out these wet events.

Synchronized swimming

Teams of synchronized swimmers perform complicated routines in deep water in time to music, and each other. Swimmers must be graceful and technically correct. Originally called water ballet, the sport was invented in Canada.

PWC racing

Personal water craft (PWC) racing is fast, fun, and exciting. Competitors compete in offshore races around set courses or perform tricks and stunts in a freestyle contest.

Dragon boat racing

Dragon boat racing originated in China and has been around for over 2,000 years. Each brightly colored dragon boat has a drummer who beats a drum so the team of 20 rowers paddle at the same time.

Underwater hockey

In this underwater version of field hockey, two teams of six players use sticks to hit the puck into the opponent's goal. Players take turns diving under the water to challenge for the puck.

Water polo

Water polo is a fast and competitive sport. Two teams of seven players aim to pass and throw the ball into the opponent's floating goal. The game can be very physical both above and below the water.

Waterskiing

Waterskiers are pulled by speed boats and have to perform impressive jumps and acrobatic tricks. There are several different types of skis, including wakeboards and trick skis.

Kite surfing

This is similar to surfing, but instead of relying on big waves, surfers use a huge kite to pull them through the water. Kite surfers perform acrobatic jumps and tricks.

Combat sports

In the combat arena, some of the fittest and strongest athletes in the world strike, grapple, or use weapons against each other to decide the winner. These sports are not for the fainthearted, and there are strict rules to make the competitions as safe as possible for all who take part.

Boxing

People have been boxing for thousands of years. In ancient Greece, the sport was part of the Olympics as long ago as 668 BCE. Today, boxing has progressed from bare knuckle street bouts to a high-profile, big-money sport.

In the ring

Boxing matches, called bouts, are divided up into periods called rounds. In each round, punches are thrown and blocked as each boxer tries to knock out his or her opponent. The main punches include the simple but effective jab, hooks that are delivered to the side of the body or head, and the uppercut, where a boxer aims at an opponent's chin. Being able to defend is just as important as attacking. Boxers use their arms to protect their heads as they sway from side to side to dodge an opponent's punches.

Boxers wear mouthguards to protect their teeth.

Jargon buster

Bob and weave: when a boxer moves his or her head up and down and side to side.

Breadbasket: a boxer's stomach area.

Clinch: when one boxer holds the other to avoid being hit.

Combination: a quick sequence of punches.

Lacing: rubbing the laces of a boxing glove into the face of an opponent.

Southpaw: a boxer who stands with his or her right hand in front of the left.

Aim of the game

Boxing takes place in a ring between two boxers of similar weight.

Boxers must throw punches to score points and knock out their opponent. The opponent who is knocked out loses the bout.

The length of a bout varies. Amateurs box two three-minute rounds and professionals 10 three-minute rounds.

Boxers are not allowed to hit an opponent below the waist, on the back of the head, or on the kidneys. They also cannot use the laced part of the gloves.

A boxer can be disqualified from a bout if they break a rule.

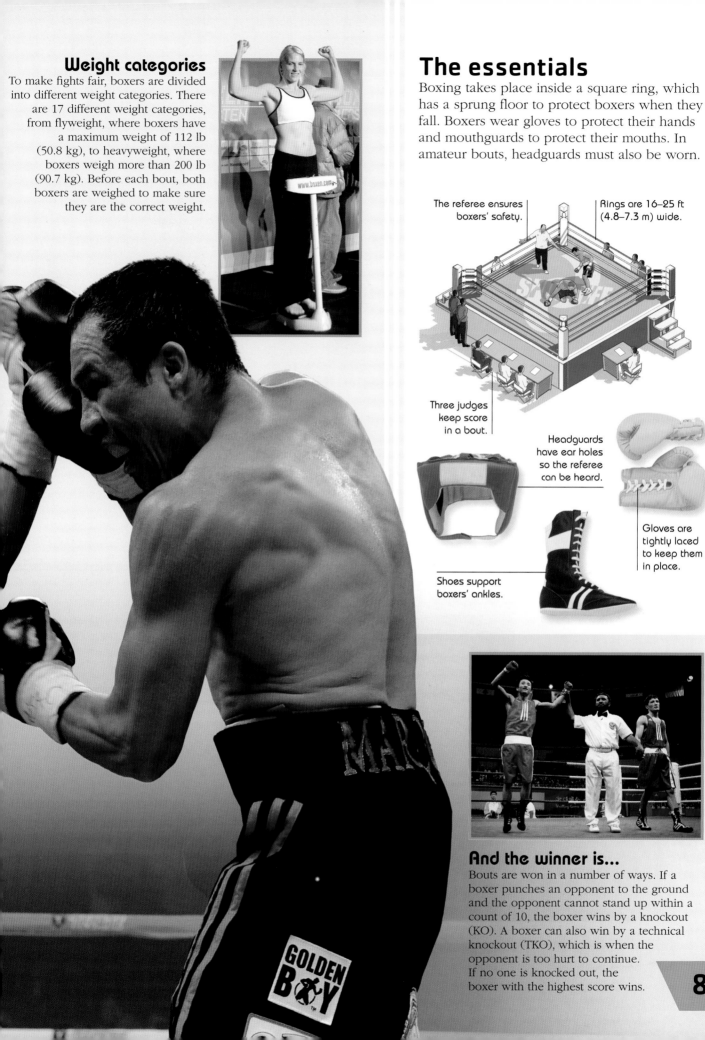

Weight categories

To make fights fair, boxers are divided into different weight categories. There are 17 different weight categories, from flyweight, where boxers have a maximum weight of 112 lb (50.8 kg), to heavyweight, where boxers weigh more than 200 lb (90.7 kg). Before each bout, both boxers are weighed to make sure they are the correct weight.

The essentials

Boxing takes place inside a square ring, which has a sprung floor to protect boxers when they fall. Boxers wear gloves to protect their hands and mouthguards to protect their mouths. In amateur bouts, headguards must also be worn.

The referee ensures boxers' safety.

Rings are 16–25 ft (4.8–7.3 m) wide.

Three judges keep score in a bout.

Headguards have ear holes so the referee can be heard.

Gloves are tightly laced to keep them in place.

Shoes support boxers' ankles.

And the winner is...

Bouts are won in a number of ways. If a boxer punches an opponent to the ground and the opponent cannot stand up within a count of 10, the boxer wins by a knockout (KO). A boxer can also win by a technical knockout (TKO), which is when the opponent is too hurt to continue. If no one is knocked out, the boxer with the highest score wins.

89

Wrestling

People have been wrestling for thousands of years, making it one of the oldest sports in the world. Many countries have their own local forms of wrestling, and they all test athletes' strength, fitness, and skill.

Grapple time

Two forms of wrestling are part of the Olympic games: freestyle and Greco-Roman. In Greco-Roman, wrestlers are not allowed to attack or touch an opponent's legs. All holds must be above the waist. Wrestlers usually use throws to get an opponent to the floor. One of the most effective throws is the shoulder throw, where the opponent is thrown over the attacker's shoulder onto the mat.

Wrestlers always wear red or blue all-in-one outfits, called singlets.

Wrestlers wear rubber-soled shoes for grip.

Takedown

Unlike Greco-Roman wrestlers, freestyle wrestlers can grab their opponents around the legs to take them to the floor. This is called a takedown. The double leg takedown is commonly used. It involves grabbing the opponent around both legs and tipping him or her to the ground.

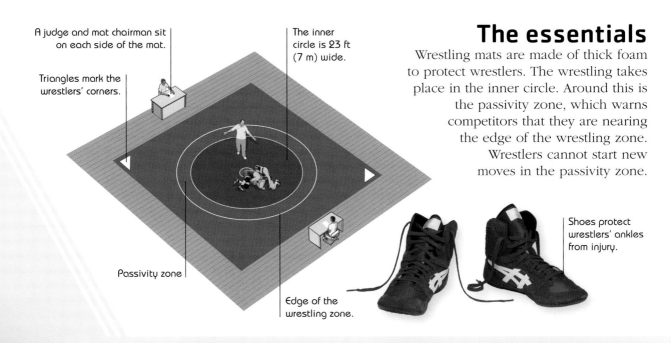

A judge and mat chairman sit on each side of the mat.

Triangles mark the wrestlers' corners.

The inner circle is 23 ft (7 m) wide.

Passivity zone

Edge of the wrestling zone.

The essentials

Wrestling mats are made of thick foam to protect wrestlers. The wrestling takes place in the inner circle. Around this is the passivity zone, which warns competitors that they are nearing the edge of the wrestling zone. Wrestlers cannot start new moves in the passivity zone.

Shoes protect wrestlers' ankles from injury.

Here, the defending wrestler in red arches her back to keep her shoulders off the mat.

Pinning to win

Wrestlers can win their matches, also known as bouts, outright if they pin their opponent's shoulders to the mat. Often bouts are not won outright and are decided by the judges' scores. Up to five points are awarded for moves such as throws and forcing an opponent to the floor.

A wide stance can stop an attempted double leg takedown.

Jargon buster

Action: the referee's command to begin wrestling.

Grapple: the holds used while opponents are standing.

Pommeling: when wrestlers grab and push each others' arms and hands to get a hold.

Reversal: when a wrestler turns a defensive position into an attacking one.

Technical superiority: a win declared when one wrestler gains a six-point lead over the other.

Judo

The word judo means "gentle way." With no kicking, punching, or weapons involved, this martial art relies on skill and cunning tactics rather than brute strength.

Floor work

After a throw, judokas compete on the floor, trying to get their opponent pinned to the mat or to submit. A judoka can be pinned by being held around the neck or the neck and legs.

On the ma[t]

Matches take place on mats called "tatami" between competitors known as "judokas." The contest area is 26 ft (8 m) wide and i[s] surrounded by the danger zone. If player[s] spend too long in the danger zone[,] they are penalized by the referee[.] Two corner judges ensure play[er] stays in the contest area[.]

The danger zone is 3 ft (1 m) wide.

The judoka in white has thrown her opponent and is forcing her to the mat.

Throws

A judo contest begins with both judokas on their feet. Each will try to get his or her opponent onto the mat by throwing them. Several throws can be used to get the opponent to the floor. Each throw uses a different body part to complete the throw. The "o-goshi" is a hip throw, while the "osotto gari" is a foot throw. In the "ippon-seoinage," the opponent is thrown over the attacker's shoulder.

Ju jitsu

Originally, ju jitsu was used to teach unarmed soldiers how to fight armed enemies. The name means "gentle art," but in reality ju jitsu is not gentle at all.

Takedown time

Ju jitsu turns an attacker's own force against himself, putting him off balance. The three main ways to do this are by striking, takedown, and submission. Strikes can be made using the hands or feet. As a strike is made, the opponent tries to use the strike to counterattack. A takedown is when the attacker throws or forces their opponent to the floor. Opponents submit if they are in a lock (where they are held by the attacker so they can't move) and can no longer stand the pain.

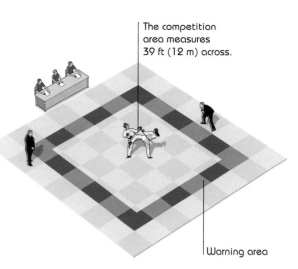

The competition area measures 39 ft (12 m) across.

Warning area

Combat zone

The inner square of the competition arena is where all the action takes place. Players must not step out of bounds. To avoid this, a warning area is set up on the edge of the fighting area. Mat referees and judges ensure that the action is safe and within the rules. A panel made up of a judge, time keeper, and scorer sit on one side of the competition area.

A clean strike is worth one point.

Aim of the game

The aim of ju jitsu is to score more points than an opponent.

Points, called "ippon," must be scored in each of the three categories: striking, throwing, and ground work.

In striking, a point is scored for a clean kick or punch.

In throwing, the attacker must make a clean takedown.

In the ground work section, the attacker must get his or her opponent to submit.

If the opponent wants to submit, he or she taps twice on the mat with a foot or hand.

Aim of the game

Karateka compete in matches, called bouts. The karateka who has the most points at the end of the bout wins.

Bouts for men last three minutes, while bouts for women and juniors last two minutes.

A referee is in charge of the bout. He or she gives a signal if the karateka has scored a point or a half point. The four corner judges help the referee to award points. The scorer keeps track of the points.

The timekeeper times the bout and stops and starts the clock at the referee's signal.

Karate

The Japanese martial art of karate is used to teach self-discipline, fitness, and spiritual awareness. Those who take part in karate are known as "karateka."

Fighting styles
There are four main styles of karate: shotokan, goju-ryu, shito-ryu, and wado-ryu. Shotokan favors strength and power. Goju-ryu karateka fight very close to each other. Shito-ryu is a combination of different styles. Wado-ryu fighters use a combination of ju jitsu and shotokan.

Gloves are worn to protect hands.

Padded boots protect karateka's feet.

Scoring a bout
Karateka fight according to gender, age, weight, and experience. They bow to each other and, when the referee gives the signal, they begin to fight by striking, kicking, and throwing their opponent. A perfect move receives a point, called an "ippon." If the move is flawed, the karateka may get a half point called a "waza-ari."

Karateka must not step into the safety area more than once.

The mat measures 26 ft (8 m) across.

Different colored belts show experience. The highest rank is the black belt.

Taekwondo

The Korean martial art of Taekwondo is one of the most popular combat sports. Competitors kick and punch each other in the head and torso to score points.

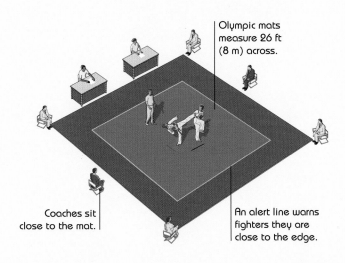

Olympic mats measure 26 ft (8 m) across.

Coaches sit close to the mat.

An alert line warns fighters they are close to the edge.

Safety first

To soften the blows, and minimize injuries, fighters have to wear protective clothing. This includes headgear, torso guards, forearm guards, and groin guards. To help the referee and judges score the match, one fighter wears red protective clothing, while the other wears blue.

Fighters wear headgear for protection.

Way of hand and foot

Each match is overseen by a referee. He or she starts and ends the match and decides if fouls are committed. The four corner judges decide if a point is scored. Blows to the torso are worth one point. Two points are scored for a kick to the head or neck. Knocking down an opponent is worth three points.

Aim of the game

Taekwondo bouts take place between two fighters over three rounds.

Fighters must kick and punch each other to score points.

The fighter with the most points at the end of the bout wins.

One fighter wins immediately and the bout is stopped if there is a knockout. A fighter also wins right away if they are 12 points ahead by the end of the second round.

Points are deducted for fouls. These include hitting below the belt, hitting the back, and hitting the back of the head.

If the scores are even, a sudden-death round is fought. The first contestant to score a point in this round wins.

The central part of the torso guard may have electronic sensors that show if a blow has been made.

Competitors are often barefoot or they may wear soft slippers.

Fencing

Modern fencing developed from sword fighting in battle. Fencers need to be fast and accurate to secure a win. Fencing is one of only four sports to appear at every modern Olympics since they began in 1896.

Aim of the game

Fencing matches are between two opponents armed with the same type of blunt sword.

A match is made up of three three-minute bouts. Competitors get a rest period of one minute between each bout.

The first fencer to score 15 points wins.

Points are scored by hitting target areas on the opponent's body. These are determined by the type of sword used.

If a competitor steps outside the back of the piste, their opponent wins a point.

Each match is overseen by a referee and jury. The jury makes sure that the fencer is not out of bounds when a touch is made.

Opponents must salute each other before and after their match as a sign of respect.

Sword play

Three types of sword are used in fencing, each of which has a safety device on its tip that registers hits. The foil is a lightweight sword with a pressure sensor on its tip. The tip must be pushed against the opponent to register a hit. An épée is heavier and stiffer than a foil and it also has a pressure sensor. The saber is the shortest sword and its tip folds back when it touches the opponent.

Face masks cover the fencer's neck and face for protection.

A fitted jacket protects against injury.

Fencers wear long black or white socks.

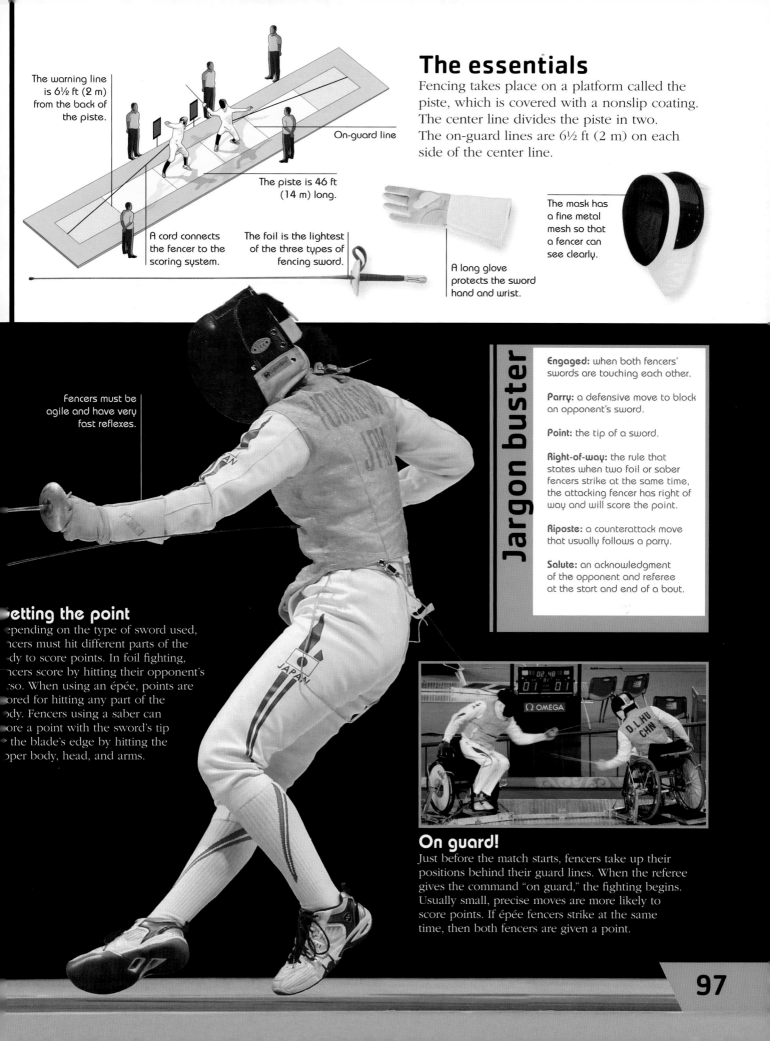

The warning line is 6½ ft (2 m) from the back of the piste.

On-guard line

The piste is 46 ft (14 m) long.

A cord connects the fencer to the scoring system.

The foil is the lightest of the three types of fencing sword.

A long glove protects the sword hand and wrist.

The mask has a fine metal mesh so that a fencer can see clearly.

The essentials

Fencing takes place on a platform called the piste, which is covered with a nonslip coating. The center line divides the piste in two. The on-guard lines are 6½ ft (2 m) on each side of the center line.

Fencers must be agile and have very fast reflexes.

Jargon buster

Engaged: when both fencers' swords are touching each other.

Parry: a defensive move to block an opponent's sword.

Point: the tip of a sword.

Right-of-way: the rule that states when two foil or saber fencers strike at the same time, the attacking fencer has right of way and will score the point.

Riposte: a counterattack move that usually follows a parry.

Salute: an acknowledgment of the opponent and referee at the start and end of a bout.

...etting the point

...pending on the type of sword used, ...ncers must hit different parts of the ...dy to score points. In foil fighting, ...ncers score by hitting their opponent's ...rso. When using an épée, points are ...ored for hitting any part of the ...dy. Fencers using a saber can ...ore a point with the sword's tip ... the blade's edge by hitting the ...pper body, head, and arms.

On guard!

Just before the match starts, fencers take up their positions behind their guard lines. When the referee gives the command "on guard," the fighting begins. Usually small, precise moves are more likely to score points. If épée fencers strike at the same time, then both fencers are given a point.

A new challenge

Combat sports require discipline and dedication. If you have this commitment then you can easily step from one combat sport to another. Here are a few you could try out.

Kendo

This Japanese sword-fighting sport is based on the ancient tradition of Kenjutsu. In addition to strict sword-fighting skills, the sport requires a high level of discipline, ritual, and etiquette.

Muay Thai

Muay Thai is a martial art that originated in Thailand. Competitors use their hands, elbows, knees, and feet to strike their opponents. Matches are decided on a points system.

Beach wrestling

Beach wrestling is a form of standing wrestling, where a wrestler tries to throw his opponent to the floor. Wrestlers fight in a sand-covered ring 6½ yd (6 m) wide.

Cage fighting

This combat sport allows fighters from different martial arts to compete against each other. It is also known as Mixed Martial Arts. Competitors try to knock out or pin their opponents while fighting in a caged ring.

Kickboxing

Kickboxing uses a mixture of boxing moves and martial arts kicks. Matches last for 12 rounds. To win, a kickboxer must knock out his opponent or score more points for hits landed.

Sumo

Sumo wrestlers can weigh over 440 lb (200 kg) and they use their weight to force their opponents off balance or out of the ring. Ritual and strategy are very important, even though matches usually last seconds.

Kung fu

Kung fu is a martial art where competitors use punches and kicks to force their opponents off a square platform, known as the lei tai. Matches are won by kickout or on points.

Winter sports

Winter sports may be held in cold conditions, but they still provide red-hot sporting excitement. The bobsled, luge, and downhill skiing are events of pure speed. Figure skating and freestyle skiing give athletes the chance to show off their artistic abilities.

Skiing

Many of the world's steepest, snowy mountains play host to skiing competitions. Some events see athletes ski down the slopes at amazing speeds. Freestyle skiers require great technical skill to perform spectacular acrobatic tricks and turns.

Alpine skiing

There are two types of alpine skiing—downhill and slalom. Downhill involves skiing from the top of a mountain to the bottom down a prepared slope called the piste. The piste has a series of widely spaced gates, which the skier must go through. In slalom, the gates are closer together to test a skier's turning ability. In the combined event, skiers do one downhill run and two slalom runs.

Tight-fitting suits help skiers go faster.

Poles help the skiers keep balanced.

Aim of the game

In alpine skiing, skiers must pass through a series of gates in the fastest time. flags on the gates show where the skiers must go next.

In ski jumping, judges award points for distance traveled and the style of skiing. The jumper with the most points wins.

In aerial skiing, each skier makes two jumps. Seven judges award points for the takeoff, length, height, form, and landing. More points are given for the difficulty of the jump. These two sets of points are multiplied together to give a final score.

Ski jumping

In ski jumping, competitors take off from a ramp and travel as far as they can. Sometimes, skiers "fly" as far as 450 ft (140 m), before trying to land as gracefully as possible. There are two lengths of ramp—90 m (295 ft) and 120 m (394 ft).

Freestyling

Freestyle events include mogul, acro, and aerial. In mogul, competitors ski down a piste that is covered with large bumps, called moguls. Mogul skiers are awarded marks for their turns, speed, and the difficulty of any tricks. Acro skiers do tricks and spins to music on a gentle slope. These skiers are judged on the difficulty and artistry of their moves. In aerial skiing, competitors jump off a ramp and perform spins and turns in midair.

Longer skis are faster, but are harder to steer.

Skiers rub wax onto their skis to help them go faster.

The essentials

A downhill piste is prepared with a layer of ice to help skiers go faster. The gates along the course are designed to spring out of the way if skiers knock them.

Ski pole

Bindings attach boots to the ski.

Ski boots support the ankles.

Helmets protect the skier against head injuries.

The electronic starting gate starts timing a skier's run.

Special netting lines the sides of the piste to catch any falling skiers.

A large clock at the finish line shows the skier's time.

103

Snowboarding

Spectacular tricks on a U-shaped half-pipe and action-packed downhill races make snowboarding one of the most thrilling snow sports for competitors and spectators.

Pads protect half-pipe snowboarders' knees.

Helmets minimize head injuries.

Aim of the game

Snowboarders compete either on a specially made half-pipe or on a snow-covered mountain slope.

Half-pipe snowboarders aim to stay on their boards as they perform acrobatic tricks in front of five judges.

Three judges mark the tricks and another two mark the overall routine out of 10.

Each boarder has two runs in which to impress the judges and score points.

In boarder-cross and slalom, the boarder who crosses the finish line first or with the fastest time wins.

Boarder-cross competitors are not allowed to push or bump each other out of the way.

In giant slalom, races are split into heats. In the first heat, riders who crash, miss a gate, or fail to finish are given a time penalty. If it happens in the second run, their opponent wins.

Heaven is a half-pipe

In trick snowboarding, competitors use the side slopes of a half-pipe ramp to make big jumps. This is called "getting air" and it allows the boarders to perform tricks as they fly above the rim of the half-pipe. Snowboarding tricks include spins and turns, such as the alley oop, which is a turn of 180 degrees in the air. Boarders also perform grabs, where they bend their knees to grab their boards in midair. In an indy grab, the boarder is upside down when he or she makes the grab.

The slopes of a half-pipe are banked, while the bottom is flat.

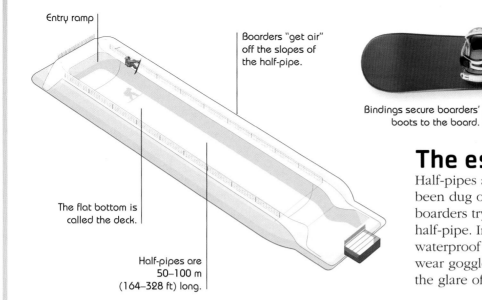

Entry ramp

Boarders "get air" off the slopes of the half-pipe.

The flat bottom is called the deck.

Half-pipes are 50–100 m (164–328 ft) long.

Bindings secure boarders' boots to the board.

The essentials

Half-pipes are U-shaped ramps that have been dug out of the snow. In competitions, boarders try to use the whole length of the half-pipe. In addition to loose-fitting waterproof clothes, many half-pipe boarders wear goggles to protect their eyes from the glare of the snow.

Four boarders compete at the same time in a boarder-cross race.

Boarder-cross and slalom

Snowboarders also compete in races. In boarder-cross, competitors race down a hill on a course marked with jumps, bumps, and huge turns. In snowboard slalom, boarders race down a mountain through special gates. Giant slalom involves a boarder racing against a rival at the same time down matching parallel courses.

Freestyle boarders slide down rails to perform tricks.

Slopestyle

In slopestyle boarding, competitors snowboard through a course of natural and artificial obstacles. These include jumps, boxes, and rails. Boarders must use these obstacles to perform tricks. Judges award scores for the tricks before deciding on an overall winner.

Bobsled

One of the fastest sports at the Winter Olympics, bobsled sees two or four athletes squeeze into a pod and hurtle down a course at 100 mph (160 kph).

Down the mountain

A race starts with the team members out of the bob. They push it along at the start and jump in before it travels down the track. Bobsled courses are usually 1,200–1,300 m (1,300–1,400 yd) long. At top competitions, such as the World Championships, they can be 1,500 m (1,640 yd). The course has turns and loops as well as straights. The turns require great skill to stop the bob hitting the walls, as this would slow it down or result in a crash.

The start is up to 54 yards (50 m) long.

Teams dismount at the finish.

Courses are made of concrete half-pipes covered in ice.

The walls are higher on bends so the bob does not come off the track.

The fiberglass bob and helmets protect the team.

Aim of the game

Bobsled teams of two or four athletes use a bob to travel as fast as possible down a course.

The race is timed from the start until the nose of the bob crosses the finish line. Each team has two or four runs. The team with the fastest time wins.

Teams are ranked before each competition and the highest ranked team goes first. When all the teams have raced once, the starting order is reversed for the second run, so the team that raced last goes first.

If a team member does not make it into the bob off the start, the team is disqualified.

Push, drive, brake

Each person in the bob has a specific task. The person at the front steers the bob and picks out the fastest route down the course. The person at the back is the brake man who stops the bob at the end of the run. In a four-person team, the other two members help to push the bob at the start of the race.

Luge and skeleton

Competitors in the luge and skeleton need nerves of steel to succeed. Traveling feet-first or face-first around a course on a metal sled is not for the fainthearted.

Skin-tight suits increase speed.

The luge

In the luge, competitors hurl themselves around a bobsled course on a sled feet-first. Athletes start by sliding back and forth while holding rails on the side of the course. With a final pull, the athlete heaves the sled off the start before lying down. Luges do not have brakes, so athletes use their shoes to slow down at the end of a race.

Only the metal runners underneath the luge are in contact with the ice.

Aim of the game

Luge and skeleton athletes must travel as fast as possible down the course. The athlete with the quickest time wins.

There are luge races for single athletes or pairs.

Athletes in the singles' competition have two runs around the course. Pairs have four attempts to record their lowest combined time.

Skeleton athletes have two attempts to record the lowest combined time possible.

The combined weight of the skeleton athlete and the sled must not exceed 254 lb (115 kg) for men and 203 lb (92 kg) for women.

Skeleton run

Athletes in the skeleton lie face-first on a sled. The sled is made of fiberglass or steel and has blades that touch the ice. Bumpers at the front and back protect the athlete from hitting the side of the course. To start, athletes push the sled forward as fast as they can, before leaping on top of it.

Skeleton athletes tuck their bodies in tight so that they go faster.

Speed skating

Skaters have been racing since the 19th century. Today, the sport is very competitive, with skaters using sophisticated equipment and perfect technique to speed over the ice.

Round and round

There are two different speed-skating disciplines: long track and short track. The long-track rink is 400 m (437 yd) and two competitors race against the clock. Short-track events involve up to six skaters racing at speeds of around 80 mph (50 kph) to cross the finish line first.

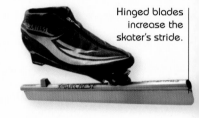

Hinged blades increase the skater's stride.

Blocks mark the edge of the rink.

Each lap of a short-track circuit is 111 m (120 yards) long.

Close quarters

Long-track skaters race in lanes, swapping lanes at the end of each circuit. The skater who starts on the inside lane wears a white armband and the skater in the outside lane wears a red armband. The short-track circuit does not have lanes. As skaters compete for the best racing line, there are often dramatic collisions and overtaking moves.

Skaters wear skin-tight suits to help increase their speed.

Skaters wear helmets and goggles for protection.

Ice skating

Ice skating is highly technical and elegant to watch. Skaters move gracefully over the ice and use spectacular turns, spins, and jumps to impress the judges and spectators.

Aim of the game

There are two forms of ice skating—ice dance and figure skating. In both of them, ice skaters are awarded points for how well they perform a routine.

The scoring system includes points for technical skill, choreography, and timing of the skating.

Points are deducted for any mistakes or illegal moves.

In figure skating, a routine must have eight compulsory moves. These include a double axel, flying sit spin, and double and triple jumps. Couples must also include spirals and throws.

Spins are an important feature of figure skating.

Balancing act

Figure skaters perform as individuals or in pairs. At competitions, they complete two routines. The first one is a short technical routine that includes eight set elements. The second routine is known as a free skate, where they must balance technical elements and creative flair.

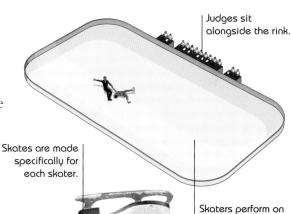

Judges sit alongside the rink.

Skates are made specifically for each skater.

Skaters perform on an unmarked rink.

Dancing on ice

Ice dancing is performed in pairs to music. At competitions, skaters perform three different routines: a compulsory dance, an original dance, and a free dance. The skaters are marked on how well they move to the music and the quality of their steps. Ice dancing routines do not include complicated lifts and spins.

Dancing pairs wear matching decorative costumes.

109

Fresh snow

Winter sports make the most of the ice and snow. They are fast and exciting. If you have mastered the art of skiing and want a new challenge, then check out these winter events.

Bandy

This winter sport is similar to ice hockey, but uses a small bright ball instead of a puck. Players use curved sticks and try to score goals. Bandy has only 18 rules and can be very high scoring.

Skibob

A skibob is a bike chassis with skis instead of wheels. It is a fast sport with skiers reaching speeds of up to 120 mph (195 kph). Skibob riders compete in downhill and slalom events.

Sled hockey

Sled hockey allows competitors with physical disabilities to play ice hockey. Sled hockey sticks are shorter than ice hockey sticks, and have metal teeth at one end to help players propel and steer their sled.

Ski flying

This winter sport is an extreme version of ski jump. Ski flyers use bigger jumps than ski jumpers and the K-point (where jumpers aim to land) is at least 200 yd (185 m) from the base of the jump.

Nordic combined

Nordic combined challenges skiers at two different ski events—ski jumping and cross-country. Skiers compete in the ski jump first, and their position then affects their starting position for the cross-country race.

Snowshoeing

Competitors wear small snowshoes and participate in races. There are many distances, from short sprints to long endurance races. There are even competitions where snowshoers race over hurdles.

Biathlon

Biathlon is a test of stamina and precision. Competitors race around a cross-country course that has one or more rifle-shooting ranges. After skiing, competitors have to shoot at targets 55 yd (50 m) away.

Horse sports

Humans and horses have been partners for thousands of years. Horse sports push this partnership to the edge. Jockeys and riders need to control and trust their four-legged friends as they are put through their paces in races and matches of raw speed, minute precision, and awesome power.

Horse racing

The thrill of thundering hooves brings millions of people to race courses around the world. They come to watch horses and riders battle to be first across the line.

On the flat

Flat horse racing takes place on a level track over a set distance. Race distances are measured in furlongs. One furlong is equal to 220 yd (201 m). The horses run on grass or an artificial, all-weather surface. The condition and hardness of the track is called "the going." The going is usually described as firm, good, soft, or heavy.

In jump racing, the fences are around 4 ft 6 in (1.4 m) high.

Aim of the game

Horse racing sees each horse ridden around a racetrack by a rider called a jockey.

Horses are identified by the jockeys' colored outfits, called silks. The colors are picked by the owners of the horse. Each owner has his or her own unique colors.

Horses of a similar age and experience race against each other.

Jockeys are not allowed to raise their whips over their shoulders. This rule stops them from hitting the horse too hard.

Stewards watch races to make sure rules are followed and that jockeys race safely.

Over the jumps

In jump racing, jockeys and their horses must clear obstacles that are placed around the course at regular intervals. There are hurdle and steeplechase races. Hurdlers must clear a set of identical fences, known as gates. Steeplechase races feature a combination of jumps including plain fences, water jumps, and open ditches. In water jumps, the horse lands in water. In an open ditch jump the ditch is on the takeoff side.

Polo

Historians believe that polo was played as long ago as 600 BCE in Persia. The sport is action-packed and fast-paced and players need to be excellent riders.

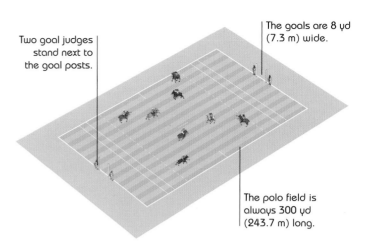

Two goal judges stand next to the goal posts.

The goals are 8 yd (7.3 m) wide.

The polo field is always 300 yd (243.7 m) long.

Keeping it safe

Players use a long mallet to hit a hard ball. This makes accidents and injuries very likely, so players wear protective helmets and knee guards. Horses are protected by bandages on their legs and a piece of equipment called a martingale. This stops a horse from lifting its head too high and injuring itself and the player. Horses' manes are shaved or braided so they are not in the way of the rider.

Knee guards protect players.

Mallets are 48–54 in (122–132 cm) long.

Helmets have chin straps so they stay on.

Field of play

Polo is played on a flat grass field the size of nine soccer fields. There are goal posts at each end of the field. A game is made up of six periods called chukkers. Each chukker lasts seven minutes. There is a break of four minutes between chukkers. Two umpires on horses and a referee on a raised platform oversee the game.

Players may change horses during the breaks between chukkers.

Aim of the game

Two teams of four horse riders compete in a game of polo.

Players use mallets to hit the ball up the field to score in the opponent's goal. The team that scores the most goals wins.

Teams swap ends after each goal has been scored.

No substitutions are allowed unless a player or horse is injured.

Players wear a position number on their shirts. Number one is the most forward attacking player and number four is the most defensive player. Number three is usually the captain and often the team's best player.

Polo balls are 4½ in (11.5 cm) in diameter.

115

Show jumping

Show jumpers are skilled riders who steer their horses around a course of obstacles. They also need to be brave to jump over tall obstacles at speed.

Jumping arena

A show jumping course can have up to 13 different obstacles, called jumps. Oxers are jumps with two sets of poles that are set next to each other to make the jump wider. An open water obstacle is a large ditch filled with water. Horses are not allowed to touch the water as they jump over.

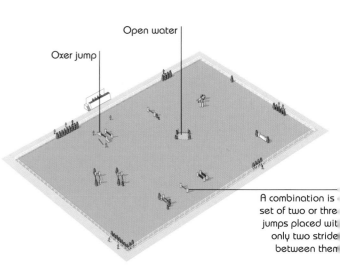

Open water

Oxer jump

A combination is a set of two or three jumps placed with only two strides between them.

Clearing a round

Riders must jump the obstacles cleanly. If a horse knocks over a fence, stops in front of one (called a refusal), or ducks past it, then riders are given four penalty points. Riders are eliminated if they fall off the horse, collect two refusals, follow the wrong route, or do not cross the start or finish line.

Aim of the game

Show jumpers ride horses around a course of jumps.

Male and female riders compete against each other.

Riders must jump over all the obstacles in the correct order and without knocking any over.

If several riders jump all the obstacles cleanly, then the winner can be decided in two ways. Either the rider with the fastest time wins, or the riders enter a jump-off. This is held over a shortened circuit and against the clock.

Eventing

Riders are tested to the limit in eventing. They need to be highly skilled in three disciplines to win. These are dressage, cross-country, and show jumping.

Dressage

In the dressage, riders use quiet commands, called "aids," to get their horses to do a series of movements. The movements include walking, trotting, and cantering, which must be completed in a set order. In the final round, the rider chooses what he or she will show the judges and the program is set to music.

Aim of the game

Eventing takes place over three or four days. Riders compete in dressage, cross-country, and show jumping.

Each event has its own rules and scoring system. In the three rounds of the dressage, riders are given a mark out of 10 from each of the five judges.

In cross-country and show jumping, riders are penalized for refusals, run-outs (where the horse ducks past a jump), and exceeding the time limit.

The rider with the highest score at the end of the competition wins.

Riders also earn points for their team. The team with the highest total number of points wins.

Cross-country

Cross-country takes place on a course of obstacles over about 3.7 miles (6 km) of countryside. Riders are expected to jump the obstacles cleanly and gallop through water hazards. If the horse or rider falls, they are eliminated from the competition.

There can be up to 45 obstacles to jump over in cross-country.

Cross-country jumps can be combinations of steep drops, banks, log barriers, and water ditches.

Wheels and motors

Sports on wheels are fast and action packed. The challenge is set for riders and machine to race and move as one, because even the slightest error can mean second best. Add an engine into this nail-biting mixture and you get high-octane moments, explosive speed, and some out-of-this-world clashes.

Formula 1

Formula 1 is a very competitive sport. Drivers race some of the most advanced cars on the planet at speeds of 220 mph (350 kph) and more.

Aim of the game

In Formula 1, a number of teams compete in races held over an entire season. Each team can have two drivers.

Drivers earn points for themselves and their teams at each race, depending on where they finish. The driver with the most points at the end of the season wins the drivers' championship. The team with the most points wins the constructors' title.

Racing takes place over three days. The first day is for practicing. Qualifying is held on the second day, when drivers try to record a fast lap of the circuit. The drivers with the fastest lap times in qualifying begin the race near the front of the starting lineup, called the grid. The race is held on the third day.

In the race, the first driver to complete a set number of laps around the race circuit wins.

Total control

Every second counts in Formula 1, and drivers need the car controls at their fingertips. The steering wheel in a Formula 1 car is covered with buttons and switches that allow drivers to control every part of the car. From the steering wheel, the driver can change gears, alter the amount of fuel going into the engine, and talk to his mechanics.

Digital display shows information about the car, including speed.

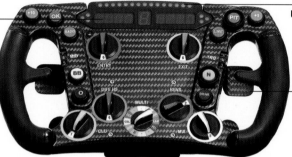

Lights help drivers to time their gear changes.

Steering wheels can be pulled out of the car so drivers can get in and out of their seats.

Drivers change gear using these paddles.

Car design

Each race team builds its own car while sticking to the rules laid out by the sport's governing body, the International Automobile Federation (FIA). Cars are equipped with powerful engines, but the engines used by different teams vary slightly, depending on the technology they are using. Cars are also given slightly different shapes to make them go faster and save vital fractions of a second.

Special wings on the car push it down into the track, increasing its grip and helping it to take corners faster.

Cars are equipped with different tires to suit different weather conditions.

Indycar

Indycar racing is packed with superfast action, as drivers battle to win dramatic races. The series features the Indy500, one of the most famous races in the world.

In the pits

At any time during a race, a driver can stop the car to change tires and refuel. These are called pit stops. Once the car has stopped, six mechanics rush to get the pit stop completed as quickly as possible so that the driver can get back into the race. Four mechanics change the tires, while the other two refuel the car.

It takes between 10 and 14 seconds to change the tires and refuel an Indycar.

Aim of the game

There are two drivers in each Indycar team.

Drivers aim to be first to cross the finish line after racing a set amount of laps around the track.

Drivers score points depending on where they finish in the race. The points are added up over the season to decide the championship winner.

During qualification, drivers race against the clock in a time trial. The faster they finish, the higher up the grid they start.

Indycar races use rolling starts. This means the cars are already moving when they start the race.

Oval circuits have banked corners, where the outside edge is higher than the inside. These allow the cars to travel faster around the corners.

To reduce the distance raced, drivers keep as close to the inside of a track as possible.

Circuits

Indycar races take place on different types of track. An oval track, which may have banked sides, is known as a speedway. Races are also held on circuits with straights, corners, and bends, just like Formula 1. These are known as street circuits—some of them are even laid out on actual city streets, such as São Paulo, Brazil, and Long Beach, California.

121

Rallying

Flying over bumps and ditches, skidding on ice, and drifting around corners are all part of the exciting sport of rally driving. Drivers speed along roads, dirt tracks, and even deserts, aiming to get to the finish line as quickly as possible.

Aim of the game

Rallying involves a crew racing a car on roads or across off-road terrain.

The race is divided into different stages or legs. Drivers must complete the stages as quickly as possible. Each stage has points along its route where the drivers' times are recorded. These are called checkpoints.

Before the race, the crew spends some time checking the race route. They do two runs of each stage. During the first run, they make pace notes. On the second run the co-driver reads the notes back to the driver.

During the check, drivers must obey a speed limit. On the day before the rally, crews are allowed to test the car in a shakedown where there is no speed limit.

Judges check cars before and after a race to ensure that they meet the correct standards.

A spoiler is fitted to the back to help the car go faster.

A radio keeps the driver in touch with his or her mechanics, who are at the finish line.

All weather, all terrain

Rallies take place throughout the year in countries around the world. As a result, drivers must be able to race in all weather conditions and over all types of terrain. These range from extreme heat and uneven roads, to snow-covered, icy lanes. Cars are modified to suit the conditions and to ensure the drivers are kept safe.

To give the drivers better grip on snowy roads, special snow tires are put on the cars.

At the controls

Unlike other motorsports, rally cars have a crew of two—the driver and the co-driver. The two must work together at all times. While the driver must be highly skilled, he must also have complete trust in his co-driver. During the race, the co-driver tells the driver what to expect on the course, such as how sharp the turns are or which obstacles are coming up.

Built to race

Rally cars may look like normal cars, but they have been altered to make them superquick and very safe. To increase their speed, the engine is made more powerful and the interior is completely stripped out to make the cars lighter. A cage of strong metal bars, called the roll cage, is installed inside the car to make it safe. The car's body is strengthened so much, it could support the weight of 10 normal cars.

Rally cars are equipped with specially shaped seats to fit the driver and co-driver perfectly.

Co-drivers give directions to the driver during the race.

Off-road

Off-road rallies are tests of endurance in some of the most extreme places on the planet. Drivers race each day over a period of time, such as a week. There is no set race route, but drivers must start and finish at fixed points and pass through checkpoints on the way.

The Dakar Rally takes drivers through scorching deserts in Africa or South America.

Rally cars are usually equipped with a turbocharged engine.

Rally cars can accelerate from a standing start to 60 mph (100 kph) in about three seconds.

Jargon buster

Crew: the driver and co-driver of a rally car.

Pace notes: the co-driver's notes that are taken during the pre-race check. They will have details of the terrain, the sharpness of bends and corners, and any obstacles to expect.

Shakedown: the official test session that takes place before the rally.

Spoiler: a special wing that helps a car move through the air more easily and go faster.

Standing start: starting from a stationary position.

Turbocharger: A device that sucks air into an engine, making it more powerful.

Motorcycles

Racing motorcycles at speeds of more than 200 mph (320 kph) requires huge amounts of skill and nerves of steel. Motorcycles do not have a shell to protect the riders, so safety is very important in all types of motorcycle racing.

Aim of the game

Motorcycle racing sees riders on the same type of bike racing around a course or a circuit.

Racers must complete a set amount of laps around the circuit. The biker to do this first wins the race.

Engine sizes range from 125 cc to 800 cc in motoGP, and from 800 cc to 1,200 cc in superbike racing.

If there is a problem with a rider's bike, the rider must pull off the circuit and park his bike where the marshal tells him.

At the start of a race, riders line up in a formation, called the grid. Their position on the grid depends on how well they did in qualifying. In off-road racing, there are no grid starts and riders start in one large group.

In races where there are pit lanes, riders must follow the set speed limit while in the pits.

Road racing

Racing takes place on circuits or roads that are closed to other vehicles. Some circuits have more uphill sections and sharp bends, while others have longer straights. Road racing includes grand prix (GP) and superbike. GP bikes are specially designed one-of-a-kind bikes, but superbikes are regular road bikes that have been modified to make them more powerful.

Leather suits have built-in knee sliders to protect riders when cornering.

Riders lean over so that they can take a bend or corner as quickly as possible.

The essentials

With riders sitting on top of a fast-moving bike that is full of fuel, safety is very important. Bikers wear full leather suits, gloves, and, most importantly, a helmet to protect themselves from injury.

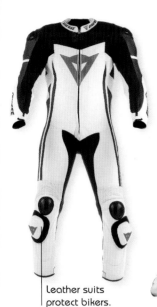

Leather suits protect bikers.

Thick gloves protect hands.

Helmets have face protectors and built-in screens, called visors.

Bikes have wide tires to give them more grip.

Off-road

Off-road motorcycle racing takes place on cross-country tracks or mud circuits. Off-road racing includes motocross (MX), supercross, and speedway. MX takes place on an outdoor circuit with drops, climbs, jumps, and straights. Supercross is an indoor version of MX. Speedway involves four riders racing around an oval dirt track. Speedway bikes are not equipped with brakes and the riders have to slide their bikes around the bends to stay in control.

The tires on MX bikes are bumpy to give the bikes as much grip on the track as possible.

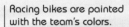

Racing bikes are painted with the team's colors.

Gravel traps on the edge of the circuit slow bikes down if they come off the track.

Safety first

In addition to wearing protective clothing, bikers must follow rules to keep them safe while racing. Circuits are also designed to be as safe as possible, with "gravel traps" and barriers to take the impact of a crash. Race marshals stand around the track, waiting to help if a rider has to leave the race or if there is an accident.

Drag racing

Drag racing is a simple test of speed. Dragsters are cars and bikes that have been specially built or altered to make them more powerful. They travel so fast that they need parachutes to slow them down.

Drag bikes

The motorcycles used in drag racing are equipped with special bars behind their rear wheels. These are called wheelie bars. They stop the bikes from flipping over as they accelerate away from the start line. With the front wheel off the ground for much of the race and only one wheel gripping the track, the bikes are extremely difficult to control.

Top fuel cars can reach speeds of 330 mph (530 kph), and reach 100 mph (160 kph) in 0.8 seconds.

Drag types

There are several different types of dragster. The fastest are called Top Fuel dragsters. These are specially built for drag racing and have wings at the front and back to improve their grip. Pro-stock cars are normal cars that have been modified so that they can complete a race in six seconds. Funny cars have a lightweight body and look a little like normal cars, but underneath the body, these powerful machines are nearly as fast as their Top Fuel cousins.

Top Fuel cars have a long slim body, with fat rear wheels and narrow front wheels.

From start to finish

Each race has a standing start. Cars line up on the staging area and wait for the lights, which are called the Christmas tree, to start the race. Drivers then accelerate down the straight track. At the end of the course, there is a deceleration area that is one-and-a-half times the length of the track. Drivers use the brakes and parachutes to stop the car in this area.

Cars are equipped with parachutes to slow them down at the finish.

Dragster safety

Dragsters use fuels that can burn very easily, such as nitromethane and methanol. Combined with very high speeds, this makes drag racing a very dangerous sport. Drivers wear flame-resistant outfits and cars are equipped with fire extinguishers and engine cutoff switches. These turn off the engine if an accident happens.

Jargon buster

Bye run: a race that sees one dragster race on its own.

Deceleration: slowing down.

Dragstrip: another name for the straight course that drag races are held on.

Nitrous oxide: also known as laughing gas. It is added to the fuel to make an engine more powerful.

Speed trap: the device used to measure a dragster's speed as it crosses the finish line.

Wheelie: when the front wheels of a car or bike lift off the ground as it pulls away from the start.

Two cars race against each other on a track with two lanes.

Aim of the game

Cyclists aim to finish a track or road race in the quickest time possible.

Some very long road races are known as tours. They are broken up into different stages. The cyclist who finishes the tour with the lowest overall time across every stage wins.

Stages in a tour contain short sprints and hill climbing races. The cyclist with the most sprint points at the end of the day wears a green jersey. The best climber wears a red and white polka-dot jersey.

All cyclists must wear helmets.

Track cyclists are not allowed to ride bikes equipped with brakes or gears.

Cycling

There are many different cycle events, some for individuals, others for teams. Cyclists need to use clever tactics to outsmart their rivals, whether their race is a short sprint on the track or a long road race.

Track cyclists wear specially shaped helmets to help them cut through the air and go faster.

Track time

Track races include short sprints and long endurance events. Sprint races include time trials and match sprints. In time trials, cyclists are timed over a set distance—the rider with the fastest time wins. In match sprints, two cyclists race against each other and the first across the finish line wins. Endurance events include pursuit races for teams or individuals and the Madison, which is a long-distance team race.

Some cyclists are known for being good hill climbers, leaving the others trailing as they power up the slope.

On the road

Road racing is a test of stamina and tactics. Some races are set in different locations, including flat city roads or mountains. The longest tour races, such as the Tour de France, feature a variety of locations that test the cyclists' sprinting, hill climbing, and fitness to the limit.

A cycle track is 250 m (273 yards) long.

The track can be made from wood, concrete, or artificial materials.

Banked corners are higher on the outside than the inside.

Light frames help cyclists to go as fast as possible.

Track bikes have no brakes.

The essentials

Track cyclists race on oval-shaped tracks. They use bikes that are designed especially for the track. These bikes have only one fixed gear, which means cyclists must pedal continuously until the bike stops. Road bikes usually have several gears and brakes.

In the team pursuit, two teams of four riders start on opposite sides of the track. They try to catch each other or finish a set distance in the fastest time.

Staged races

Many tour races feature teams of riders. Teammates work together to ensure their team's lead rider wins the stage or finishes as close as possible to the winner. If the lead rider is a good sprinter, the team will work to keep up with the other cyclists during the race. When they are close to the finish, the lead rider can break away from the others and use his or her pace to win the stage.

Jargon buster

Individual pursuit: an endurance race where cyclists start on opposite sides of the track and try to catch each other or be the first to complete a set distance.

Kierin: a race where riders sprint to the finish after completing a set number of laps behind a motorcycle called a derny.

Madison: a race over 50 km (31 miles) for teams of two or three riders. Riders get points for winning short sprints within the race.

Peloton: the main group of cyclists in a tour race.

Sprint finishes are common in tours. Every second counts toward the cyclists' overall tour time.

Mountain biking

One of the newest Olympic sports, mountain biking sees cyclists race over muddy tracks and up and down steep, tree-covered hills and mountains.

Long-distance races

Many mountain bike races are 20–30 miles (30–50 km) long and are held on specially prepared countryside circuits. Some races are even longer. Marathon events can be 60 miles (150 km) long, while enduro races see teams of two or four riding constantly for up to 25 hours.

Mountain bikes are fitted with shock absorbers, which give the cyclist a smoother ride.

Downhill

Racing downhill requires a great deal of courage. Downhill mountain bikers ride down very steep slopes that have bumps and jumps and huge drops. Mountain bikers wear helmets and body armour in case they tumble and fall.

Helmets protect the face from loose dirt and stones.

Tires have bumps for added grip.

BMX

The first BMXs were built in the 1960s to race over off-road dirt tracks. Today, track racing is an Olympic sport and freestyle is contested at urban competitions.

Track racing

Eight riders compete in a BMX track race. The race track is usually 330–440 yd (300–400 m) long and the best cyclists will take less than one minute to complete it. Tracks feature bumps, jumps, and banked corners, where the outside of the track is higher than the inside.

BMX track racers wear helmets to protect them from serious head injuries.

Bikes are made from lightweight metals.

Wheels are 20 in (51 cm) across.

Aim of the game

In track racing, the first cyclist over the line wins the race.

A race meeting usually has a series of qualifying races, called motos. The most successful cyclists then race in a series of ride-offs. These end in a grand final, which produces the overall winner.

Track bikes must meet certain guidelines, such as they must have license plates and cannot have chain guards.

Flags are used to communicate with riders. A green flag means the track is unobstructed and racing can continue. A yellow flag means the course is obstructed. A red flag tells riders to stop and return to the start.

In freestyle BMX competitions, the biker with the highest score wins the competition.

Freestyle

Trick BMX cycling is called freestyle. Competitions take place on specially made ramps, called vert ramps, across urban landscapes, or on a flat surface (called flatland). Bikers are scored by a panel of judges and they are given marks for their skill and the difficulty of the tricks they perform.

Bikers launch themselves into the air off steep ramps called vert ramps.

Skateboarding

The first skateboards were made in the 1940s. Since then, boarding has become one of the world's most popular street sports. Today, boarders can practice their craft in skateparks, where they perform tricks using specially made ramps.

Vert skaters launch themselves high into the air to perform tricks.

Helmets are worn in half-pipe contests.

Getting air

Vert skating is a type of skateboarding that is performed on a U-shaped ramp called a half-pipe. Boarders skate up and down the sides of the ramp to gain speed. When they are traveling fast enough, they take off. This is known as "getting air." It allows the boarder to perform tricks. The tricks include jumps, such as the grab 540, where the boarder grabs hold of the board and turns one-and-a-half times in the air before landing.

Freestyle boarders skate over street furniture, such as railings and stairs.

Using obstacles

Not all competitions take place in a skatepark. In street boarding, boarders skate over street curbs, rails, and steps. To get over obstacles on the street course, boarders use special tricks such as the ollie. In an ollie, the boarder pushes down on the tail of the board, flipping the board up to clear an obstacle.

Skateboarding can be enjoyed by individual boarders anywhere, from streets to skateparks.

In trick competitions such as vert or street, skateboarders have a set amount of time to score as many points as possible.

In vert competitions, points are awarded for the difficulty and the height of tricks—the higher the trick, the more points scored.

Points are scored for the number of times a boarder spins before landing. The more spins and turns, the higher the points the boarder scores.

In some street competitions, boarders ollie over as many cones as they can. More cones means more points.

At the end of the competition, the boarder with the most points wins.

Some boarders race each other in downhill competitions. Competitors can reach speeds of 75 mph (120 kph).

Trucks and wheels

The main parts of a skateboard are the deck, trucks, and wheels. The deck is the board the skateboarder stands on. It is made from thin layers of wood glued together. The wheels are fitted to trucks, which are fixed underneath the board. The wheels are usually made of plastic. Smaller wheels are better for performing tricks, while larger ones make the board more stable.

The essentials

Most boarders wear baggy, comfortable shorts, T-shirts, and flat-soled sneakers. They also wear helmets and knee and elbow pads for protection. Some boarders also use wrist strappings to prevent sprains.

Helmets help to minimize injury.

Pads protect elbows and knees from injury.

Boarders put grip tape on the deck.

The back of the board is the tail.

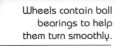
Wheels contain ball bearings to help them turn smoothly.

Trucks allow the boarder to rock from side to side to turn the skateboard.

Power on

A sport can be fast when it's motor-powered! Competitors have to be skilled athletes and learn to master a machine. Here are some action-packed wheel and motor sports that are exciting to watch and take part in.

Air race
Pilots fly light aircraft through slalom-style gates, known as air gates. The tricky courses make the pilots fly low, loop, and dodge around obstacles. The fastest through the course wins.

World superbike
The motorcycles used in world superbike are adapted road bikes. Each round has two races and the riders' points are added together to decide the best rider and motorcycle manufacturer.

Inline skating
There are two categories of inline skating: speed and aggressive. Speed skaters race around a track. Aggressive skaters perform tricks and stunts.

Stock car racing
This is a full-contact motor sport. Cars are allowed to bump and push each other as they race around an oval track. In the US, the sport is known as NASCAR and includes the famous Daytona 500 race.

Go-karting

A great starter sport for budding Formula 1 drivers, go-karting involves racing karts around a twisting track. Superkarts can reach speeds over 155 mph (250 kph), although amateur karts are slower.

Truck racing

This unusual sport involve trucks racing around circuits similar to those used in other track-racing events. For safety reasons, trucks aren't allowed to go above 100 mph (160 kph).

Isle of Man TT

This prestigous motorcycle race has been held on the Isle of Man, UK, every year for more than 100 years. The race is a time-trial format, where riders race against the clock around the closed-off public roads.

Extreme sports

Extreme athletes like to take things to the limit—and then push things a little further. In the search for more and more exciting sports, athletes have developed more extreme forms of competition. These include leaping out of planes, jumping off cliffs, and racing through some of the most dangerous parts of the planet.

Free diving

Instead of using breathing apparatus, free divers hold their breath as they dive under water. Top free divers can reach depths of more than 300 ft (90 m), holding their breath for longer than three minutes at a time.

Dive lines measure how deep divers go.

Aim of the game

Free divers aim to stay under water for as long as possible, going as deep as they can on just one breath.

Free diving is done by individuals rather than teams.

Divers may wear fins to help them ascend.

Nose clips are worn to help divers cope with the pressure that builds up in their ears as they dive deeper.

Free diving can take place in a pool or in open water, including lakes, rivers, and the ocean.

Constant weight divers and free immersion divers must ascend wearing whatever weights they used to descend.

Wet suits help to keep divers' bodies at a constant temperature.

In a pool
Static and dynamic free diving takes place in a swimming pool. Static divers descend face down, holding their breath for as long as possible. Dynamic divers swim horizontally under the water to descend as deeply as possible.

Dive lines can be used to pull out a diver in an emergency.

Coming up for air
There are different types of free diving in open water, including constant weight, free immersion, variable weight, and no limits. The biggest difference between them is how divers descend (go down) and ascend (come up). Constant weight divers descend using weights. Free immersion divers use a dive line to descend and ascend. In variable weight and no limits diving, divers use a sled to descend.

Cliff diving

As long ago as the 1170s, Hawaiian warriors were diving off cliffs to show their bravery. Today, fearless divers perform acrobatic leaps off towering cliffs and platforms around the world.

Divers need strength and bravery to do acrobatic tricks off a cliff.

Step into the unknown

Most cliff diving takes place off natural cliff faces. Often divers will dive directly off the cliff, but sometimes a platform is used. If this is the case, the platform must be 3 ft (1 m) out from the cliff face. For competitions, the cliff face must be 75–92 ft (23–28 m) high for men and 59–75 ft (18–23 m) high for women. The water below the cliff must be at least 16 ft (5 m) deep.

Dives

In a competition, cliff divers must make a series of acrobatic twists and turns during a dive. Judges give marks for the takeoff, the acrobatics, and the entry into the water. The takeoff is marked for its height and the diver's angle. The tricks are scored on how difficult they are and how well they are performed. Divers must enter the water with as little splash as possible.

Divers lose points if their legs open during a dive.

Aim of the game

Cliff divers dive off a cliff face or platform to perform acrobatic tricks before hitting the water.

In competitions, there are usually three rounds. Divers are allowed just one dive per round.

Five judges mark the divers, each one giving the diver a mark out of 10.

The highest and lowest scores are ignored and the rest are added together. This total is then multiplied by a score for the difficulty of the dive to give a final score.

At the end of the competition, the diver with the highest points wins.

Skydiving

Jumping out of an airplane with a parachute strapped to your back is not for everyone. However, skydiving competitions see experienced parachutists not only jumping out of the plane, but also performing tricks and acrobatic moves with teammates.

Helmets help to prevent head injuries in an accident.

Leaving the plane

Skydivers usually dive in clear skies. Once they have left the plane, they fall toward the ground in a free fall. Often they fly face-first, known as "belly-to-earth" and perform tricks or formations. Skydivers open their parachutes so that they are fully open when the divers reach 2,500 ft (760 m). The open chutes enable them to float down to the ground, where they land in an area called the drop zone.

Skydivers jump from their airplanes at a height of 13,000 ft (4,000 m).

Formation diving

Skydivers take part in formation diving in teams of four, eight, or more. In competitions, the formation dive lasts 35 seconds for teams of four or 50 seconds for larger teams. Teams must complete set formations as many times as possible in the time allowed. Each team also has a free fall videographer who films the dive for the judges to see and award points. Canopy formation sees skydivers open their parachutes as soon as they leave the plane. They then perform moves as they descend, including linking together to create a stack of parachutes.

Freestyling

In freestyle events, solo skydivers perform acrobatic moves, such as rolls and tumbles, before opening their parachutes. Freeflying is another skydiving discipline. It sees skydivers perform tricks while falling in positions other than belly-to-earth. These positions include head-down flying, stand-ups, and sit flying, as if the skydiver is in a chair.

Freestyle skydivers usually jump with a partner, who films the moves using a camera on a helmet.

Aim of the game

In competitions, skydivers come together in formations, or complete tricks before opening their parachutes.

Skydiving competitions usually take place over six to 10 rounds—each round is one jump.

Competition dives are filmed and shown to judges, who give the skydivers scores.

Formation divers score a point for each successful formation they complete. The team with the most points at the end of the competition wins.

In freestyle and freeflying skydiving, skydivers are given points based on the precision, difficulty, and creativity of the performance. They are also marked on the quality of the camera work.

Once skydivers reach an altitude of 2,500 ft (760 m), they open their parachutes and glide back to the drop zone on the ground.

Skydivers have a second parachute, called the reserve, which they use if the first one fails.

Skydivers hold their arms and legs out wide to keep themselves stable during the free fall.

The essentials

Skydivers wear a harness system, called a rig, strapped to their bodies. Inside the rig are the divers' two parachutes. Altimeters tell divers how high above the ground they are. Because divers fall at speeds of about 120 mph (190 kph), eye protection and helmets are essential.

Altimeters can be strapped to the chest or wrist.

Goggles allow the skydivers to see clearly during the fast free fall.

Parachutes have steering lines so skydivers can steer them to the drop zone.

Freeride mountain bikers use a specially designed bike to go down a mountain.

In competitions, all riders start at the top of the same mountain.

Once passing through a starting gate, they can choose whatever route (called a line) they like to get down the mountain. They must go through a finishing gate at the bottom.

Riders are judged on their choice of lines down the course, their technical ability, and the difficulty of any tricks.

Freeride mountain biking

The only rule in freeride is that there are no rules! Freeride combines elements of downhill and big-jump biking. Bikers can use whatever means they have to get down the mountain.

Jumping helps bikers get down the hills quickly and with style.

All terrains

There are no set freeride trails—freeriders use deep countryside, unused ski slopes, downhill courses, or artificial urban courses in towns and cities. On a typical course, a freerider must jump over or ride through obstacles. These can include anything from raised narrow tracks to jumps or rivers.

Comfy ride

Originally, freeride mountain bikers rode modified downhill bikes. Today, freeride bikes still look similar to downhill bikes, but they are usually smaller and lighter. They are equipped with rear and front suspension to give the bikers a more comfortable ride over rough ground.

Suspension protects the rider over rough ground.

Powerful brakes are essential.

Knobby tires give good grip.

142

Ultra-running

A normal marathon is 26 miles (42 km) long, but ultra-marathons can be three times as long. They are also held in some of the harshest places on the planet.

Comfort is key

In addition to comfortable running shoes and lightweight clothing, runners wear a race number for easy identification. Those competing in colder temperatures and snow need to keep warm, but must be careful not to become too hot and uncomfortable. In sun or snow, runners usually wear sunglasses to protect their eyes from the glare of the landscape.

Shoes protect athletes' feet.

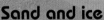

Keeping hydrated is vital.

Aim of the game

Runners must complete a course. Whoever finishes the race in the quickest time wins.

Some ultra-running races are over a set distance, such as 50 km (31 miles). Others take place over a specific time period, such as 24 hours or even six days.

Runners must race on their own power, carrying their own equipment. This may include a GPS system, water or drinks bottles, and snacks.

Runners cannot use artificial cooling systems.

Runners must check in with race organizers at certain intervals.

Sunglasses and hats protect runners from the sun.

Sand and ice

Ultra-running races can take place anywhere, from roads to deserts. Some races are held in difficult conditions such as searing heat or freezing cold. One of the best-known ultra-marathons is the Four Deserts. Runners race 156 miles (250 km) over the Sahara, Gobi, and Atacama deserts, before running in Antarctica.

Antarctica's freezing cold is the final challenge for runners in the Four Deserts race.

Extra extreme

There are many more adrenaline-fueled activities that push athletes to their limits. Some are so high-risk they can only be done by people over the age of 18.

Paragliding

Paragliders use a special parachute, known as a paragliding wing, to catch air currents and soar over the countryside. They are towed into the air by airplanes or jump off the sides of hills and mountains.

BASE jumping

BASE jumpers leap off tall objects with just a parachute and a lot of nerve. BASE stands for the places they jump from: Buildings, Antennae, Spans (such as bridges), and Earth (such as cliffs).

Parkour

This urban sport uses street apparatu such as railings, walls, and steps, to perform acrobatic moves with speed and skill. Also known as freerunning it started life in Paris and has grown in popularity around the globe.

Hang gliding
Strapped to a harness below a large rigid wing, competitors launch themselves off a cliff or mountainside into the wind. Some hang gliders have reached altitudes of up to 16,000 ft (4,875 m).

Street luge
Much like its parent sport luge, competitors use a special sled with wheels to race down slopes—not of ice, but mountain roads. Sleds can hurtle along at speeds of up to 95 mph (155 kph).

Free climbing
Free climbing is an extreme form of mountain climbing, where climbers scale rockfaces without safety ropes. They rely on their strength and skill to climb challenging mountainsides.

Whitewater kayaking
This sport takes kayaking to the extreme as competitors race over river rapids (fast-flowing water that crashes over rocks and other obstacles). Rapids are graded from 1 (easy) to 6 (dangerous). Some kayakers also perform tricks.

Olympic Games

Athletes from all around the world compete for glory at the Olympic Games—the world's greatest sporting event. They train for years with the goal of winning a gold medal for their country. The three modern Olympic competitions: Summer, Winter, and Paralympic Games are watched and enjoyed by audiences of billions.

SUMMER SPORTS

Archery
Badminton
Basketball
Beach volleyball
Boxing
Canoe/Kayak slalom
Canoe/Kayak sprint
Cycling—BMX
Cycling—mountain bike
Cycling—road
Cycling—track
Diving
Equestrian—dressage
Equestrian—eventing
Equestrian—show jumping
Fencing
Gymnastics—artistic
Gymnastics—rhythmic
Gymnastics—trampoline
Handball
Hockey
Judo
Modern pentathlon
Rowing
Sailing
Shooting
Soccer
Swimming
Synchronized swimming
Table tennis
Taekwondo
Tennis
Track & field
Triathlon
Volleyball
Water polo
Weightlifting
Wrestling

WINTER SPORTS

Biathlon
Bobsled
Curling
Figure skating
Ice Hockey
Luge
Skeleton
Skiing—alpine
Skiing—cross-country
Skiing—freestyle
Skiing—Nordic combined
Ski jumping
Snowboarding
Speed skating

US swimmer Michael Phelps
has won 16 Olympic medals,
including eight golds won at
Beijing in 2008.

147

Olympic history

The earliest Olympic Games were held by the ancient Greeks nearly 3,000 years ago. Today's Olympics are truly international. Athletes from 205 countries will compete for more than 300 gold medals at the 2012 London Olympics.

At the 1936 Berlin Games, Jesse Owens broke five world records.

The ancient games

The first Olympic Games were held in 776 BCE. Like the modern games, they were held every four years and events included running, jumping, chariot racing, and wrestling. These ancient games lasted until about 400 CE, when they were banned by the Romans.

The ancient games took place in honor of the Greek god Zeus. Men would gather on Mount Olympus to test their sporting skill.

The modern Olympics

Throughout the 19th century, people tried to revive the Olympics. In 1894, Frenchman Pierre de Coubertin succeeded and set up the International Olympic Committee (IOC). Today, the IOC is still responsible for organizing the Games. The first modern Games took place in Athens in 1896. They have since been held in some 40 different cities around the world, including London (1908 and 1948), Melbourne (1956), Tokyo (1964), and Atlanta (1996).

Australian swimmer Ian Thorpe won five gold medals at the 2000 Sydney Games and the 2004 Athens Games.

Game on (and off)

Since 1896, the modern Olympic Games have been held every four years and canceled only three times—in 1916, because of World War I, and 1940 and 1944, because of World War II. More recently, some countries have chosen not to attend the games for political reasons. In 1980, the United States and some other countries did not go to the Games in Moscow, while the Soviet Union and many of its allies chose not to go to the next Games in Los Angeles in 1984.

Olympic heroes

The record for the most Olympic medals won by one athlete is held by Soviet gymnast Larissa Latynina. She won a total of 18 medals: six in Melbourne in 1956, six in Rome in 1960, and six in Tokyo in 1964. Latynina is one of only four athletes to have won nine gold medals. She is also one of only three female athletes to have won the same event at the summer Games three times.

Medals

Athletes who win their Olympic event are crowned Olympic champions and win a gold medal. The second-place athlete gets a silver medal, and the athlete who comes in third receives bronze. They are given their medals at a special ceremony. A medals table shows how many medals each country has won, so countries can see how successful they have been.

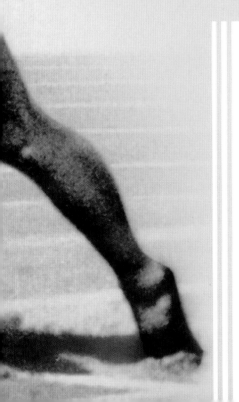

Medal winners stand on the podium to receive their medals.

Summer Olympics

Every four years, billions of people tune in to watch the Olympic action unfold. Athletes dream of winning gold, while spectators hope to see world records broken and history made.

Individuals

The Summer Olympics can be divided into individual and team sports. Events for individuals include tennis, archery, cycling, track & field, and swimming. Some of these sports also include team events. Athletes and swimmers compete in team relays, while cyclists race in a team pursuit. In some sports, such as eventing, individual success also counts toward a team medal.

Gymnasts compete individually, but there is also an overall team event.

Olympic heroes

Usain Bolt was the track star of the 2008 Beijing Olympics. Not only did he win the 100-meters gold medal, but he also managed to smash the world record. In the final of the 200 meters, Bolt went on to break Michael Johnson's long-standing world record by 0.02 seconds. Then, together with Nesta Carter, Michael Frater, and Asafa Powell, the Jamaican 4 x 100 m relay team won the gold medal, breaking the world record, and making it three wins out of three for Bolt.

The main Olympic stadium is the focus of the Summer Games and the site of the track & field events.

Team sports

Water polo, field hockey, basketball, and synchronized swimming are just some of the Olympic team sports. With national pride at stake, each member of the team must perform at their best. In some sports, pairs of athletes must work as a team.

Water polo was first played at the 1900 Olympics.

New sports

If a sport is played around the world and meets certain criteria, it may become an Olympic sport. Some of most recently added sports include triathlon, which was added in Sydney in 2000, and BMX racing, which was added in Beijing in 2008.

Rugby sevens will be played for the first time at the 2016 Rio Olympics.

Host cities

The Games bring more than 10,000 athletes to the host city, as well as thousands of spectators. Cities bid to host the games and once they win the bid, the hard work begins. Stadiums have to be built or improved and an Olympic Village for athletes is also constructed.

	1896	Athens, Greece
	1900	Paris, France
	1904	St. Louis, United States
	1908	London, United Kingdom
	1912	Stockholm, Sweden
	1920	Antwerp, Belgium
	1924	Paris, France
	1928	Amsterdam, Netherlands
	1932	Los Angeles, United States
	1936	Berlin, Germany
	1948	London, United Kingdom
	1952	Helsinki, Finland
	1956	Melbourne, Australia
	1960	Rome, Italy
	1964	Tokyo, Japan
	1968	Mexico City, Mexico
	1972	Munich, West Germany
	1976	Montreal, Canada
	1980	Moscow, Soviet Union
	1984	Los Angeles, United States
	1988	Seoul, South Korea
	1992	Barcelona, Spain
	1996	Atlanta, United States
	2000	Sydney, Australia
	2004	Athens, Greece
	2008	Beijing, China
	2012	London, United Kingdom
	2016	Rio de Janeiro, Brazil

Winter Olympics

Originally, some winter sports were included at the Summer Games. This changed in 1921, when the International Olympic Committee (IOC) approved a Winter Sports Week to take place in 1924 in Chamonix, France. Afterward, this week became known as the first Winter Olympics.

On the slopes

The Winter Olympics feature several snow sports that take place on the mountain slopes. The cross-country skiing and Nordic combined (cross-country skiing and ski jumping) contests took place at the first Winter Olympics, and alpine skiing was added in 1936. Both men's and women's snowboarding first took place at the Nagano Games in 1998 with a giant slalom competition. In 2002, parallel giant slalom was added, while in 2006, snowboard cross also made its debut.

Alpine skiing includes slalom and giant slalom, as well as downhill.

Olympic heroes

Magdalena Neuner is a three-time Olympic medal winner. The German biathlete took part in her first Olympic Games in Vancouver in 2010 and earned the nickname "Gold Lena." She won gold in the pursuit and mass start races and silver in the sprint.

Curling appeared at the very first games but was dropped. It reappeared at Nagano in 1998.

On the rink

The Olympic ice rink hosts curling, ice hockey, and various skating events. Both curling and ice hockey are team sports—the only other Winter Olympics team sport is bobsled. Speed skating, figure skating, and ice dance are all part of the Olympic skating program.

On the run

Three of the fastest ice sports take place on the bobsled course. These are bobsled, luge, and skeleton. Men's bobsled took place at the first-ever Winter Games, but an event for women was not added until 2002. Although skeleton was contested at the 1928 Games, it was dropped and reappeared only in 2002 at Salt Lake City. Luge has been an Olympic sport since 1964.

The first Olympic half-pipe competition took place at the Nagano Games.

To the extreme

Not all snow sports take place on mountain slopes. The half-pipe snowboard competition takes place on a specially built half-pipe ramp. Boarders use the ramp to get as high as possible to do tricks. Ski jumpers launch themselves off an ice ramp, while each freestyle ski contest has its own special course.

Hosting the Winter Games

Originally, the Winter Games were held in the same year as the Summer Games. This changed in 1986, when the IOC voted to hold the Winter and Summer Games in different years. To make this program work, there were Winter Games in Albertville in 1992 and Lillehammer in 1994. After that, the Winter Games followed their own four-year program.

1924	Chamonix, France
1928	St. Moritz, Switzerland
1932	Lake Placid, United States
1936	Garmisch-Partenkirchen, Germany
1948	St. Moritz, Switzerland
1952	Oslo, Norway
1956	Cortina d'Ampezzo, Italy
1960	Squaw Valley, United States
1964	Innsbruck, Austria
1968	Grenoble, France
1972	Sapporo, Japan
1976	Innsbruck, Austria
1980	Lake Placid, United States
1984	Sarajevo, Yugoslavia
1988	Calgary, Canada
1992	Albertville, France
1994	Lillehammer, Norway
1998	Nagano, Japan
2002	Salt Lake City, United States
2006	Turin, Italy
2010	Vancouver, Canada

Paralympic Games

In 1948, disabled patients at Stoke Mandeville Hospital in the UK took part in a sports competition. Four years later, the competition included athletes from other countries, and so the Paralympics was born. Today, athletes with many kinds of disability compete at the Games.

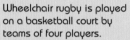

Wheelchair rugby is played on a basketball court by teams of four players.

Specific sports

Some sports, such as goalball and boccia, appear just at the Paralympics. Goalball, which is similar to volleyball without a net, is played by visually impaired athletes. Boccia is like bowls. It is played by wheelchair athletes with cerebral palsy.

The Paralympics

The name "Paralympics" stands for "parallel Olympics," because they are held alongside the main Olympic Games. Since 1992, the Paralympics have taken place at the same venues as the Summer and Winter Olympics. Olympic cities must take the paralympians and their sports into account when designing facilities.

SUMMER PARALYMPIC GAMES

	1960	Rome, Italy
	1964	Tokyo, Japan
	1968	Tel Aviv, Israel
	1972	Heidelberg, West Germany
	1976	Toronto, Canada
	1980	Arnhem, Netherlands
	1984	Stoke Mandeville, United Kingdom and New York, United States
	1988	Seoul, South Korea
	1992	Barcelona, Spain
	1996	Atlanta, United States
	2000	Sydney, Australia
	2002	Salt Lake City, United States
	2004	Athens, Greece
	2008	Beijing, China

WINTER PARALYMPIC GAMES

	1976	Örnsköldsvik, Sweden
	1980	Geilo, Norway
	1984	Innsbruck, Austria
	1988	Innsbruck, Austria
	1992	Albertville, France
	1994	Lillehammer, Norway
	1998	Nagano, Japan
	2002	Salt Lake City, United States
	2006	Turin, Italy
	2010	Vancouver, Canada

On the track

Many Olympic sports have been modified for the Paralympics. Some have new rules—for example, volleyball is played by athletes who sit on the floor. Other sports, such as tennis and basketball, have been modified to accommodate athletes in wheelchairs. Many sports have different categories, depending on the athlete's disability.

Vision impaired soccer players wear eye patches to ensure they all have the same lack of vision. The ball has a bell so that players can hear where it is.

Categories

Each Paralympic event is divided into categories so that athletes compete against others with similar disabilities. There are six general categories, including amputees and wheelchair users. The goal is to make the event as fair and as competitive as possible.

Track athletes with different disabilities have separate races.

Paralympic heroes

Known as "the blade runner," South African athlete Oscar Pistorius runs on carbon fiber prosthetic limbs. At the 2008 Beijing Summer Paralympics, Pistorius won the gold medal in the 100 meter, 200 meter, and 400 meter track events. In addition to breaking world records in those distances, he also earned a new nickname: "the fastest man on no legs."

Winter Games

There are five different sports in the Winter Paralympics. Alpine skiing (including slalom), Nordic combined (cross-country skiing and ski jumping), and cross-country skiing take place on the mountainside. Wheelchair curling and sled hockey take place on an ice rink.

Amputees ski the slalom on the same slopes as the able-bodied skiers.

Glossary

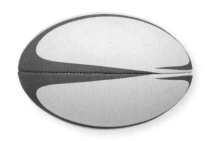

Apparatus
The equipment artistic gymnasts use to perform their routines such as vaults, balance beams, and pommel horses.

Armed
To have a weapon.

Attacker
A type of player in a team who tries to score goals or points.

Bout
A combat sport match.

Backhand
A stroke played in a racket sport that is made with the back of the hand facing outward and the arm moving forward.

Banked
Sloped or inclined. For example, an Indycar circuit has banked turns.

Binding
The fittings on a snowboard or ski that secure the boots to the board or ski.

Carbon fiber
A lightweight but very strong material made from carbon.

Cue ball
The white ball in pool or snooker that players hit first using a cue. This, in turn, hits the colored object balls.

Defender
A type of player who tries to stop the opposition attackers from scoring.

Delivery
In baseball and cricket, a ball that is thrown by the pitcher or bowler at a batter or batsman. In bowls, and ten-pin bowling, it is used to describe how a person rolls or throws the ball.

Diamond
The infield playing area of a baseball game that includes the three bases and home plate.

Endurance
To do something for a long time.

Extra time
The time added on to the end of a game or match.

False start
Starting a race before the whistle is blown or the starter's gun is fired.

Fiberglass
A lightweight material made from extremely fine glass fibers woven together. It is used to make equipment, such as luge sleds and surfboards.

Forehand
A stroke played in a racket sport where the player's palm is facing the direction of the stroke.

Handover
When an athlete in a relay race passes the baton to his or her teammate, who continues the race.

GPS
Short for global positioning system. An electronic system that helps people to find out where they are.

Grid
The starting position of vehicles in a motorsports race. The vehicle that qualifies in the fastest time starts at the front of the grid, while the slowest vehicle starts from the back of the grid.

Half-pipe
A U-shaped ramp used to perform tricks. Skateboarding, BMX, and snowboarding all have half-pipe contests.

Hardcourt
An artificial surface, usually asphalt or concrete, on which tennis is played. The surface is covered in a layer of rubber and it is usually painted blue or green so that players can see the ball.

Hazard
An obstacle, such as a bunker or stream, found on a golf course.

Header
When soccer players use their heads to strike the ball.

Infringement
Breaking a rule of a sport.

Intercept
When a player catches or blocks a ball that was thrown or passed between two opposition players.

Knockout
When a boxer punches his or her opponent to the ground and the opponent cannot get up again.

Mechanic
A person who fixes cars or motorcycles. In motorsports, several mechanics can work on one vehicle at a time.

National sport

A sport that is so popular in a country that it is part of the country's culture. For example, ice hockey is the national sport of Canada.

Nordic combined

A snow sport where competitors take part in cross-country skiing and ski jumping.

Object ball

The colored balls in a game of pool or snooker.

Olympic sport

A sport played at the Olympic Games. Sports must meet certain criteria to become Olympic sports.

Olympic Village

The accommodation and other facilities built for the thousands of athletes taking part in the Olympic Games.

Open water

Rivers, lakes, or the sea. Windsurfing, free diving, and swimming contests can take place in open water.

Out line

The line that marks the top edge of a squash court. Hitting over this line means that the ball is out.

Qualifying

In motorsports, a pre-race time trial in which a driver or rider's time determines their starting position on the grid or starting line. In other sports, such as swimming or track and field, competitors may have to reach a certain standard or time in a qualifying race, or heat, to take part in the final race or competition.

Race marshal

A race track official whose main job is to ensure the safety of the competitors and spectators around the track.

Rally

An exchange of strokes in a court game, such as tennis, squash, or volleyball, that ends when one team or player fails to make a good return. Usually this results in a point being scored or the loss of service.

Rank

A measure of how well a player or team performs. The number-one ranked player is the best.

Refusals

In eventing and show jumping, when a horse refuses to jump over a fence. Riders are penalized for refusals.

Return

To hit the ball back to an opponent or opposing team after a service.

Rink

The ice on which ice hockey, curling, and skating sports take place. Lawn bowls is also played on a rink of cut grass.

Runs

The unit of scoring in baseball and cricket. In baseball, a run is scored when a batter hits the ball and either he or another player on the batting team crosses home plate. In cricket, a single run is scored when a batsman hits the ball and successfully runs to the other end of the field.

Slalom

A type of race where competitors must pass through special gates on their way to the finish line. There are slalom races in skiing, snowboarding, and kayaking competitions.

Smash

In racket sports, a shot that is hit from high up and brought down onto the court or table, often resulting in winning a point.

Solo

A single competitor or to do something by oneself.

Spectators

The people who watch a sport, either live at the event or on television.

Spikes

The shoes worn by track athletes that have spikes on their soles.

Snooker

When a snooker player blocks an object ball with another ball so that the opponent cannot hit the object ball with a direct shot.

Submission

In combat sports, such as jujitsu, when a competitor feels he or she cannot continue and gives up.

Tactics

A team or individual sportsperson's plans for reaching a goal.

Triathlon

A sporting contest in which competitors compete in three events—swimming, cycling, and running.

Videographer

A person who films something. In skydiving, each team has a videographer who films the action.

Wet suit

A special suit worn by sportsmen and women who take part in water sports, such as sailing and free diving. The wetsuit keeps them warm.

Index

A

acro skiing 103
acrobatics 55
aerial skiing 102, 103
air races 134
alpine skiing 102, 152
archery 66–7
Australian rules football 22–23

B

badminton 35
bandy 110
BASE jumping 144
baseball 12–13
basketball 14–15
beach fighting 98
beach soccer 11
beach volleyball 16
biathlon (winter sports) 111, 152
bikes 128–31
    BMX 131
    cycling 128–129
    mountain biking 130
billiards 69
BMX 131
boarder-cross 105
bobsled 106, 153
boccia 154
Bolt, Usain 150
boules 68
bowling, ten-pin 62–63
bowls 61
boxing 88–9
    kickboxing 99

C

cage fighting 98
cliff diving 139
climbing, free 145
Coubertin, Pierre de 148
cricket 26–27
croquet 68

cross-country
    eventing 117
    running 45
    skiing 152
curling 60
cycling 128–129

D E

Dakar Rally 123
darts 69
discus 48
distance running 44–45
diving 74–75
    cliff diving 139
    free diving 138
drag bikes 126
drag racing 126–127
dragon boats 84
dressage 117
English billiards 69
eventing 117

F

fencing 96–97
field events 46–49
field hockey 25
fighting
    beach fighting 98
    cage fighting 98
figure skating 109
five-a-side soccer 11
floor gymnastics 54–55
football 18–19
Formula 1 120
Four Deserts Race 143
free climbing 145
free diving 138
freeride mountain biking 142
Futsal 29

G

go-karting 135
goalball 154
golf 58–59
Greco-Roman wrestling 90
gymnastics 52–55, 149, 150

H

hammer 49
handball 29
hang gliding 145
high jump 46
horse racing 114
horse sports 112–117
horseshoes 69
hurdling 43
hurling 28

I

ice dancing 109
ice hockey 24
ice skating 109
Indycar 121
inline blades 134
Isle of Man TT 135

J

Jai-alai 38
javelin 48
ju jitsu 93
judo 92
jump racing 114
jumping (track & field) 46–47

K

karate 94
karting 135
kayaking 77
    whitewater 145
kendo 98
kickboxing 99

ite surfing 85
ung-fu 99

M

acrosse 39
atynina, Larissa 149
ong jump 46
uge 107, 153
    street luge 145
Marathon 44
    ultra-marathon 143
nartial arts
    ju jitsu 93
    judo 92–93
    karate 94
    taekwondo 95
nogul skiing 103
notocross (MX) 125
notorcycle racing 124–125
    drag bikes 126
    Isle of Man TT 135
    World Superbike 134
nountain biking 130
    freeride 142
Muay Thai 98

N O

etball 17
Neuner, Magdalena 152
Nordic combined 111, 152
Ocean racing 78
Olympic Games 146–155
open-water swimming 72
Owens, Jesse 148

P

oaddleball 38
paragliding 144
Paralympic Games 154–155
oarkour 144
oetanque 68
Phelps, Michael 147
oickelball 39
oing-pong 34
oistol shooting 69
Pistorius, Oscar 155
oole vault 47
oolo 115

pool (target sports) 65
powerlifting 51
PWC racing 84

R

racquetball 38
rallying 122–123
real tennis 39
rhythmic gymnastics 54
rifle shooting 68
road racing
    cycling 128
    motorcycles 124
rowing 76
rugby sevens 151
rugby union 20–21

S

sailing 78–79
sculling 76
Sepak Takraw 29
shooting
    pistol shooting 69
    rifle shooting 68
shot put 49
show jumping 116
skateboarding 132–133
skeleton 107, 153
skibob 110
ski flying 111
ski jumping 102, 111
skiing 102–103
    Nordic combined 111
skydiving 140–141
sled hockey 110
snooker 64
snowboarding 104–105, 152, 153
snowshoeing 111
soccer 10–11
softball 28
soft tennis 38
speed skating 108
speedway 125
sprinting 42–43, 150
squash 36–37
steeplechase
    horse racing 114
    track & field 45
stock car racing 134

street luge 145
Summer Olympics 147, 150–151
sumo 99
supercross 125
surfing 82–83
swimming 72–73, 147, 149
swords 96
synchronized diving 75
synchronized swimming 84

T

table tennis 34
taekwondo 95
ten-pin bowling 62–63
tennis 32–33
    real tennis 39
    soft tennis 38
Thorpe, Ian 149
throwing (track & field) 48–49
track & field 42–49, 148, 150
track events 42–45
triathlon 44
truck racing 135
tug of war 29

U V

ultimate 28
ultra-running 143
underwater hockey 84
volleyball 16, 155

W

walking races 44
water polo 85
waterskiing 85
water sports 70–85
weightlifting 50–51
whitewater kayaking 145
windsurfing 80–81
Winter Olympics 147, 152–153
Winter Paralympics 155
winter sports 100–111
World Cup
    soccer 11
    rugby union 20
World Superbike 134
wrestling 90–91
    sumo 99

Acknowledgements

Dorling Kindersley would like to thank Fleur Star, Carrie Love, and Lorrie Mack for their editorial assistance, and Chris Bernstein for preparing the index.

The publisher would like to thank the following for their kind permission to reproduce their photographs:

Key: a–above; b–below/bottom; c–centre; f–far; l–left; r–right; t–top

1 Getty Images. 2–3 Getty Images: AFP. 4 Getty Images: Creative Crop (bl). **Courtesy of Speedo/ Brandnation:** (br). 5 Action Images: (tr). Fotolia: Claber (tl). 6–7 Getty Images: Bongarts. 7 Action Images: (cra). Corbis: Clifford White (br). Getty Images: AFP (tr, cr, crb). 8–9 Press Association Images: AP Photo/David J. Phillip. 10 Getty Images: Bongarts (cl); Ryan McVay (bl); Stockbyte (br). 11 Getty Images: Chelsea FC (br); Ryan McVay (tr); LatinContent. 12 Getty Images: Craig Veltri (br); (cl). 12–13 Getty Images. 13 Getty Images: David Madison (tr). 14 Getty Images: Fuse (br); NBAE (cl). 15 Alamy Images: George S de Blonsky (t). **Getty Images:** NBAE (b). 16 Getty Images: AFP (b, br). 17 Getty Images: (b). 18 Getty Images. 19 Getty Images: (cr, t). 20 Getty Images: Creative Crop (cl); (t). 20–21 Getty Images: (b). 21 Getty Images: (cla); Creative Crop (tc). 22 Getty Images: (r). 23 Getty Images: (tl, c), Corbis: Image Source (br). 24 Getty Images: C Squared Studios (tl); NHLI (b). 25 Getty Images: AFP (b); Thomas Northcut (tl, tr). 26 Getty Images: (c). 26–27 Corbis: Rahat Dar/epa. 27 Getty Images: AFP (t). 28–29 Corbis: Pete Stone (t). 28 Action Plus: (br). Alamy Images: Stephen Barnes/Sport (bc); Paul McErlane (bl). 29 Action Plus: (bl). Action Images: (bc, br). 30–31 Getty Images. 32–33 Corbis: Michael Cole. 32 Corbis: Adam Stoltman (bl). 33 Alamy Images: Neil Tingle (c). Getty Images: Creative Crop (bl, tr). 34 Getty Images: AFP (bl). 35 Getty Images: AFP. 36–37 Getty Images: AFP. 36 Getty Images: (bl). 37 Getty Images: (tl, br, tr). 38 Action Images: (bl). Alamy Images: Jeff Greenberg (bc). Getty Images: (br). 38–39 Action Plus. 39 Action Images: (bl, br). Alamy Images: dmac (bc). 40–41 Getty Images: LatinContent. 42–43 Getty Images: AFP. 42 Getty Images: AFP (b). 43 Getty Images: AFP (tl); Tobias Titz (br). 44 Getty Images: (br); Sports Illustrated (t). 45 Getty Images: AFP (b); (t). 46 Action Plus: (r). Corbis: Brian Garfinkel/Icon SMI (l). 47 Action Plus: (t). Action Images: (r). Getty Images: Tobias Titz (cl). 48 Getty Images: (cl, b). 49 Getty Images: (cl, tc). 50 Getty Images. 50–51 Getty Images. 51 Getty Images: Bongarts (br); (t). 52 Getty Images: (l). 52–53 Getty Images. 53 Getty Images: (t, cr). 54 Getty Images: AFP (bl). 54–55 Action

Images. 55 Getty Images: AFP (tr); (b). 56–57 Alamy Images: Gaertner. 58 Getty Images: (t). 58–59 Getty Images: (b). 59 Getty Images: (tc). 60 Getty Images: (b); Ryan McVay (ca, tl). 61 Getty Images: (c, l). 62 Getty Images: Getty Images for DAGOC (r). 63 Getty Images: Getty Images for DAGOC (tr); Doable/A.collection (cr). 64 Getty Images: Getty Images for 888.com (b). 65 Getty Images: AFP (b); Davies and Starr (t, tr). 66–67 Getty Images. 67 Getty Images: Comstock (tr); Getty Images for DAGOC (cr); David Madison (br). 68–69 Alamy Images: Caro. 68 Action Plus: (tr, bc). Action Images: (bl, br). 69 Action Images: (bl, br). Alamy Images: PhotoStockFile (bc). 70–71 Action Images. 72 Getty Images: (c). **Courtesy of Speedo/ Brandnation:** (tl). 72–73 Getty Images: AFP. 73 Getty Images: (br). **Courtesy of Speedo/ Brandnation:** (cr). 74 Action Plus: (l). 75 Action Plus: (b). Getty Images: AFP (cl); (bl). 76 Getty Images: (t, b). 77 Getty Images: (l). 78–79 Getty Images. 78 Getty Images: (b). 79 Getty Images: AFP (cr); Image Source (br). 80–81 Corbis: Juan Medina/Reuters. 80 Courtesy Starboard: (l). 81 Alamy Images: MiRafoto.com (tl). Getty Images: AFP (cr); Creative Crop (br). Courtesy Starboard: (bl/board). Tushingham Sails Ltd: (bl). 82–83 Getty Images: ASP. 82 Getty Images: ASP (bl). 83 Corbis: Frederic Larson/San Francisco Chronicle (tr). Fotolia: Jay Beaumont (br/surfboard). **Tushingham Sails Ltd:** (br). 84–85 Action Images. 84 Alamy Images: Barry Bland (br); Emil Pozar (bl). Corbis: Derek M. Allan; Travel Ink (bc). 85 Action Plus: (bl, bc, br). 86–87 Corbis: Patrik Giardino. 88–89 Getty Images. 89 Action Images: (t). Getty Images: (br). 90 Getty Images: AFP (bl); Comstock (tl). 90–91 Getty Images. 91 Getty Images: Bongarts (cr); Comstock (tr). 92 Getty Images: AFP (cl); Bongarts (b). 93 Corbis: Gong Lei/Xinhua Press (b). 94 Fotolia: Claber (tl, tr). Getty Images: AFP (br). 95 Getty Images: (b). 96–97 Getty Images. 97 Getty Images: AFP (br). 98–99 Action Images. 98 Action Images: (bc). Alamy Images: Barry Bland (br); Peter Treanor (bl). 99 Action Images: (br). Alamy Images: mikecranephotography.com (bc); Linda Richards (br). 100–101 Action Plus. 102–103 Getty Images. 102 Action Images: (br) 103 Courtesy Fischer Skis: (b). Getty Images: (cr). 104–105 Getty Images: Sports Illustrated . 105 Getty Images: (br); Sports Illustrated (c). 106 Getty Images: AFP. 107 Getty Images: (br). 108 Getty Images: Sports Illustrated (b). www. cadomotus.com/Marchese: (t). 109 Getty Images: (cl, b). 110–111 Corbis: Matthias Schrader/epa. 110 Action Plus: (bc). Corbis: Ilya Naymushin/ X01151/Reuters (bl). Getty Images: National Hockey League (br). 111 Action Plus: (bc). Corbis: Sampics (br); Erich Schlegel (bl). 112–113 Getty Images.

114 Getty Images: (b, t). 115 Getty Images: LatinContent (b). 116 Action Plus. 117 Getty Images: AFP (t); Sports Illustrated (b). 118–119 Getty Images: AFP. 120 Action Images: (b). Getty Images. Courtesy Virgin Racing: (c). 121 Getty Images: (c, b). 122 Corbis: Reporter Images/epa (bl). 122–123 Corbis: Antonio Cotrim/epa. 123 Action Images: (tl). Getty Images: AFP (cr). 124–125 Getty Images: AFP (b). 124 Action Images: (tl). 125 Action Images: (tr, tr/motorbike, cr). Courtesy Dainese S.p.A: (tl). Getty Images: (br). 126–127 Getty Images: (b). 126 Corbis: Dannie Walls/Icon SMI (c). 127 Corbis: Gene Blevins (c); Jayne Oncea/Icon SMI (t). 128–129 Getty Images. 128 Corbis: (bl). 129 Getty Images: (br). Courtesy Saddleback Ltd: Felt Bicycles (tr). 130 Getty Images: (cl, b). 131 Getty Images: AFP (cl); (b). Giant, www.giant-bicycles.com: (c). 132 Getty Images: (l). 133 Fotolia: Robert Kelsey (bl/helmet). Getty Images: (t, br). 134–135 Getty Images. 134 Action Plus: (bl, br). Corbis: Duomo (bc). 135 Action Plus: (bl). Alamy Images: Richard McDowell (bc). Getty Images: (br). 136–137 Action Plus. 138 Corbis: Franck Seguin/TempSport (br). Rex Features: Neale Haynes. 139 Action Images: (l). Getty Images: Sports Illustrated . 140–141 Getty Images: Max Dereta. 140 Getty Images: Steve Fitchett (b). 141 Corbis: Wolfgang Deuter (br). Dreamstime.com: Magmarczz (bl). Getty Images: Oliver Furrer. Kroop's Goggles: (bc). 142 Giant, www.giant-bicycles.com: (tl, bl). 143 Alamy Images: Art Directors & TRIP (ca, tr). Courtesy CamelBak: (c). Getty Images: AFP; (bl). 144–145 Corbis: Bill Ross. 144 Alamy Images: Extreme Sports Photo (br). Corbis: Uli Wiesmeier (bl); Ahmad Yusni/epa (bc). 145 Corbis: Joe McBride (bl); Galen Rowell (bc); Ty Milford/Aurora Photos (br). 146–147 Getty Images: Bob Thomas Sports Photography . 147 Getty Images: AFP (r). 148 Getty Images: Hulton Archive (l); (r). 149 Getty Images: Hulton Archive (tr); (tl, bl, br). 150 Getty Images: AFP (l); (r). 150–151 Corbis: Tim De Waele. 151 Getty Images: (c); Sports Illustrated (tr). 152 Getty Images: (bl, br). 152–153 Getty Images. 153 Getty Images: (t); Sports Illustrated (br). 154–155 Getty Images. 154 Getty Images: (cl). 155 Getty Images: AFP (t); (bl, br). 156 Getty Images: Creative Crop (t); Fuse (c). 157 Getty Images: Comstock (r). 158 Courtesy Fischer Skis: (bl). Fotolia: Aleksandr Ugorenkov (bc). Getty Images: Image Source (br). 159 Action Images: (bl) Giant, www.giant-bicycles.com: (br). 160 Fotolia: Jay Beaumont (bc); Robert Kelsey (bl). Courtesy Virgin Racing: (br).

All other images © Dorling Kindersley
For further information see: www.dkimages.com